A LITERARY BOOK *of* DAYS

A LITERARY

BOOK of DAYS

CROWN PUBLISHERS, INC. NEW YORK

Published by Crown Publishers, Inc., 201 East 50th Street, New York, New York 10022.
Member of the Crown Publishing Group.

Random House, Inc. New York, Toronto, London, Sydney, Auckland
Crown is a trademark of Crown Publishers, Inc.

Manufactured in Singapore

Picture Research: Diane Cook
Design: Louise Fili
Design Assistant: Leah Lococo

ISBN 0-517-59432-3

10 9 8 7 6 5 4 3 2 1

First Edition

Cover illustration and title page illustration by Rockwell Kent:
Courtesy of The Rockwell Kent Legacies

"We carry with us both the life that we have chosen and all the other lives we might have lead."

—KENNETH TYNAN

J A N U A R Y

1879: E. M. Forster b. London. "One always tends to overpraise a long book because one has got through it," he would later say. When a student asked him in 1966 why no other novels had followed 1924's *A Passage to India*, he said, "I have been racking my brains and can find no reply [to] this very reasonable question. I can only suggest that the fictional part of me dried up." 1915: "What a vile little diary! But I am determined to keep it this year . . . " — Katherine Mansfield, in her journal. 1919: J. D. Salinger b. New York City. Norman Mailer later calls him "the greatest mind ever to stay in prep school." 1920: Gotham Book Mart opens in New York City.

New Year's Day

1920: Isaac Asimov b. Petrovichi, Russia. 1929: Maxwell Perkins meets Thomas Wolfe to discuss the manuscript of *Look Homeward, Angel.* 1931: "Here are my resolutions. . . . First, to have none. Not to be tied. To make a good job of *The Waves*. To go out yes—but stay at home in spite of being asked. As for clothes, I think to buy good ones."—Virginia Woolf, in her journal. 1955: Of hearing his books read aloud, Osbert Sitwell confesses on NBC-TV, "It is music to my ears. I have always said that if I were a rich man, I would employ a professional praiser."

1882: When U.S. Customs asks Oscar Wilde if he has anything to declare, Wilde responds, "Nothing but my genius." 1892: J. R. R. Tolkien b. Bloemfontein, South Africa. To critics who said his writing was difficult to understand, he acknowledged, "I am told that I talk in shorthand and then smudge it." 1978: "Much of writing might be described as mental pregnancy with successive difficult deliveries."—J. B. Priestley, in the *International Herald Tribune.*

1785: Jakob Grimm b. Hanau, Germany. He would later coauthor *Grimm's Fairy Tales* (1812–1822) with his brother, Wilhelm. 1980: President Jimmy Carter and Rosalyn Carter host the first White House reception honoring poets. Attendees include James Dickey, Richard Eberhart, and Gwendolyn Brooks; Robert Penn Warren, Archibald MacLeish, and Malcolm Cowley decline.

1821: "Clock strikes: going out to make love. Somewhat perilous, but not disagreeable."—Lord Byron, in his journal. 1895: Henry James's play *Guy Domville* is booed on its opening night. He plunges into a deep depression despite good reviews from H. G. Wells and George Bernard Shaw. 1950: *The Member of the Wedding*, by Carson McCullers, based on the author's novel, opens in New York City to critical acclaim. 1980: Joy Adamson, author of *Born Free*, is killed in Nairobi. Authorities attribute her death to a lion but later speculate that she may have been murdered by human hands. 1986: Susan Sontag, writing in *The New York Times:* "The writer is either a practicing recluse or a delinquent, guilt-ridden one; or both. Usually both."

1878: Carl Sandburg b. Galesburg, Ill. "I was up day and night with Lincoln for years," he once said of his biography of Abraham Lincoln. "I couldn't have picked a better companion." 1931: E. L. Doctorow b. New York City. In 1985 he told *The New York Times*, "Planning to write is not writing. Outlining . . . researching . . . talking to people about what you're doing, none of that is writing. Writing is writing."

Left: Lord Byron *Right:* Carl Sandburg

1891: Zora Neale Hurston b. Eatonville, Fl. 1972: Poet John Berryman commits suicide at 58 by jumping into the Mississippi River.

1824: Wilkie Collins b. London. 1913: Harold Munro opens London's Poetry Bookshop, the site for the first meeting between Robert Frost and Ezra Pound. 1917: Peter Taylor b. Trenton, Tenn.

E.L. Doctorow

1873: Israeli poet Chaim Nachman Bialik b. Rady, Russia. 1882: Oscar Wilde commences his American lecture tour at Chickering Hall in New York City. Audiences in later cities mock him by waving sunflowers and calling him an "ass-thete." Once back in England, Wilde has the last word: "In America, life is one long expectoration." 1908: Simone de Beauvoir b. Paris. She once said in an interview, "Patience [is one of those] 'feminine' qualities which have their origin in our oppression but should be preserved after our liberation."

1845: After she praises his work in her poem "Lady Geraldine's Courtship," Elizabeth Barrett, 38, recieves a note from Robert Browning, a little-known poet, 32. It reads: "I love you." 1887: Robinson Jeffers b. Pittsburgh, Pa.

1903: Alan Paton b. Pietermaritzburg, South Africa. "If you wrote a novel in South Africa which didn't concern the central issues," he once said, "it wouldn't be worth publishing." 1936: Dashiell Hammett and Raymond Chandler meet in Los Angeles at a dinner for contributors to *Black Mask*.

1876: Jack London b. San Francisco. He later said, "I write a book for no other reason than to add three or four hundred acres to my magnificent estate." 1899: Oscar Wilde writes to Robert Ross, "Henry James is developing, but he will never arrive at passion, I fear."

1834: Horatio Alger b. Revere, Mass. "Horatio Alger wrote the same novel 135 times and never lost his audience," George Juergens later remarked of him. 1980: *The Times Literary Supplement* (London) revives after a year-long strike, pronouncing of Tom Wolfe's *Right Stuff:* "If there's no thesis, and the observations are untrustworthy, what's left is the wonderful Tom Wolfe style machine."

1896: John Dos Passos b. Chicago. "If there is a special Hell for writers it would be in the forced contemplation of their own works," he once said. 1925: Yukio Mishima b. Tokyo, into a samurai family. 1963: Sylvia Plath's *Bell Jar* is published. 1986: "A newspaper account tells you what happened," Nadine Gordimer pronounces. "But it's the playwright, the novelist, the poet, the short-story writer who gives you some idea of why."

1622: Molière b. Paris. 1891: Osip Mandelstam b. Warsaw. After his death in 1938 he was memorialized in his widow Nadezhda's *Hope Against Hope.* 1961: Robert Frost accepts John F. Kennedy's invitation to speak at his inauguration, replying, "If you can bear at your age the honor of being made president of the United States, I ought to be able at my age to bear the honor of taking some part in your inauguration." 1980: On the release of her first novel, Susan Cheever tells *The New York Times* of father John: "My father wasn't that rich or famous when I was growing up. He was just my father. . . . He was more of a father than the other kids' fathers, because he worked at home."

Martin Luther King, Jr.'s Birthday

1966: "Most contemporary novelists, especially the American and the French, are too subjective, mesmerized by private demons," Truman Capote tells *The New York Times.* "They're enraptured by their navels and confined by a view that ends with their own toes."

1706: Benjamin Franklin b. Boston. Once, when asked what condition of man most deserved pity, he responded, "a lonesome man on a rainy night who does not know how to read." 1902: The first issue of *The Times Literary Supplement* (London) appears.

1689: Montesquieu b. near Bordeaux, France. 1867: Nicaraguan poet Rubén Darío (born Félix Rubén Gargía y Sarmiento) b. Metapa, now Ciudad Darío. He will revolutionize Spanish poetry, bringing it into touch with the modernist movement of other languages. 1882: A. A. Milne b. London. 1939: W. H. Auden and Christopher Isherwood sail for the United States. "The most important literary event since the outbreak of the Spanish War," claims Cyril Connolly.

Cover of Horatio Alger's *Facing the World*

1809: Edgar Allan Poe b. Boston. He will be expelled from West Point in 1831 for appearing on the parade ground dressed in rule-book regalia "white belt and gloves"—but nothing else. 1887: Alexander Woolcott b. Phalanx, N.J. The model for the egotistical Sheridan Whiteside in Kaufman and Hart's *The Man Who Came to Dinner* would later be called "Old Vitriol and Violets" by James Thurber.

1961: Robert Frost, 86, recites his poem "The Gift Outright" at President John F. Kennedy's inauguration. 1993: Maya Angelou recites her stirring poem "On the Pulse of Morning" at the inauguration of President Bill Clinton, becoming the first poet to read at an inauguration since Robert Frost. The day before, she asserts: "I ask everybody to pray for me all the time. . . . Pray for me, please, for the inaugural poem. Not in general. Pray for me by name. Say: 'Lord! Help Maya Angelou.' Don't just say, 'Lord, help six-foot-tall black ladies,' or poets or anything like that. . . . 'Lord, help Maya Angelou. Please!'"

1952: William Shawn succeeds Harold Ross as editor of *The New Yorker*. 1987: Mystery writer P. D. James tells the *Los Angeles Times*, "In 1930s mysteries, all sorts of motives were credible which aren't credible today, especially motives of preventing guilty sexual secrets from coming out. Nowadays, people *sell* their guilty sexual secrets."

1561: Francis Bacon b. London. 1788: Lord Byron b. London. In his diary, the day before his thirty-third birthday in 1821, he writes, "Through life's road, so dim and dirty,/I have dragg'd to three-and-thirty;/What have these years left to me?/Nothing, except thirty-three." 1849: August Strindberg b. Stockholm.

1783: Stendhal, né Marie-Henri Beyle, b. Grenoble, France. To aspiring writers, he gives but one directive: "To be clear." 1936: George Orwell writes: "I worshipped Kipling at 13, loathed him at 17, enjoyed him at 20, despised him at 25, and now again rather admire him." 1978: "There are thousands of causes for stress, and one antidote to stress is self-expression. That's what happens to me every day. My thoughts get off my chest, down my sleeves and onto my pad."—Garson Kanin to *Publishers Weekly*.

24 1862: Edith Wharton b. New York City. She wrote the opening lines to her first "novel" at 11: " 'Oh, how do you do, Mrs. Brown?' said Mrs. Tompkins. 'If only I had known you were going to call, I should have tidied up the drawing room.' " Her mother reviewed the sample and told her daughter, "Drawing rooms are always tidy." 1987: Mona Simpson reflects on her best-selling novel *Anywhere But Here*: "I don't know for sure if the mother in the novel is a good mother or not, but I do like her. There are many noble sisters in literature, but not many mothers and daughters."

25 1759: Robert Burns, Scottish poet and songwriter, b. Ayrshire. 1874: W. Somerset Maugham b. Paris, at the British embassy. "There are three rules for writing a novel," he once declared. "Unfortunately, no one knows what they are." 1882: Virginia Stephen (later, Woolf) b. London. "I thought *nothing* of her writing," Edith Sitwell later sniffed. "I considered her a 'beautiful little knitter.'" 1950: Gloria Naylor b. New York City. She once said, "One should be able to return to the first sentence of a novel and find the resonances of the entire work."

26 1831: Mary Mapes Dodge *(Hans Brinker, or The Silver Skates)* b. New York City.

27 1832: Lewis Carroll b. Daresbury, Cheshire, England. 1931: Mordecai Richler, author of *The Apprenticeship of Duddy Kravitz*, b. Montreal.

Illustration from Lewis Carroll's *Alice in Wonderland*

Edith Wharton

28 1661: "A lady spat backward upon me by mistake [at the theater], not seeing me. But after seeing her to be a very pretty lady, I was not troubled at it at all."—Samuel Pepys, in his journal. 1873: Colette b. Saint-Sauveur-en-Puisaye, France. She got her start ghostwriting stories for her author husband, who would lock her in a room until she finished each assignment.

29 1737: Thomas Paine b. Thetford, England, the son of a Quaker corsetmaker. 1845: Edgar Allan Poe's "The Raven" appears in the New York *Evening Mirror*, earning him fame both in the United States and overseas. 1860: Anton Chekhov b. Taganrog, Russia. A friend once implored him to drop his medical practice and devote all his time to writing. "Medicine is my lawful wife and literature is my mistress," Chekhov replied. "When I get tired of one, I spend the night with the other." 1923: Paddy Chayevsky b. Bronx.

Colette, Paris, 1951

1912: Pulitzer Prize–winning historian Barbara Tuchman (*The March of Folly*) b. New York City. She would one day write, "Books are the carriers of civilization. Without books, history is silent, literature dumb, science crippled, thought and speculation at a standstill. Books are humanity in print." 1935: Richard Brautigan b. Spokane, Wash. 1985: "A thick steady snow providentially cancelled The Lunch. . . . Maybe this is part of the cantankerous pleasure of getting older and skilled at what you do. You rejoice at thick snow so you don't have to have lunch with an ass who happens, at the moment, to be an important somebody in publishing."—Gail Godwin, in her journal. 1990: On the release of his latest book, *India: A Million Mutinies Now*, V. S. Naipaul muses: "It would be nonsensical for me to write the same kind of novel I wrote 34 years ago. My theory is that Dickens was driven to an early grave by the Dickensian novel. I think he carried it like a burden. No wonder he died at the age of 58; it was too much for him."

1905: John O'Hara b. Pottsville, Pa. On the 1967 publication of his thirty-fifth book, he said, "They say great themes make great novels . . . but what these young writers don't understand is that there is no greater theme than men and women." 1915: Thomas Merton b. Prades, France. 1923: Norman Mailer b. Long Branch, N.J. "I have been running for President these last ten years in the privacy of my mind," he wrote in 1959's *Advertisements for Myself*. He realized an approximation of his fantasy ten years later when he ran for mayor of New York City, with Jimmy Breslin as a running mate and "No More Bullshit" as a campaign slogan. 1948: J. D. Salinger's wrenching short story "A Perfect Day for Banana Fish" appears in *The New Yorker*.

Anton Chekhov

F E B R U A R Y

1902: Langston Hughes b. Joplin, Mo. He was "discovered" when, as a busboy at a Washington, D.C. restaurant, he left a batch of his poems next to Vachel Lindsay's plate and slipped away. Lindsay read the poems aloud at dinner, and Hughes learned about his celebrity in the papers the next day. 1904: S. J. Perelman b. Brooklyn. "The fact is that all of us have only one personality, and we wring it out like a dishtowel," he would later say. "You are what you are." 1918: Muriel Spark b. Edinburgh, where she will set *The Prime of Miss Jean Brodie*. Of her 1984 novel *The Only Problem*, John Updike said in *The New Yorker*, "Her sentences march under a harsh sun that bleaches color from them but bestows a peculiar, invigorating, Pascalian clarity."

1882: James Joyce b. Dublin. D. H. Lawrence greeted his *Ulysses* coldly, calling it "nothing but old fags and cabbage stumps of quotations from the Bible and the rest, stewed in the juice of deliberate, journalistic dirty-mindedness." 1886: Author and journalist William Rose Benét b. Fort Hamilton, N.Y. 1905: Ayn Rand b. St. Petersburg, Russia. She wrote in 1957's *Atlas Shrugged*: "To demand 'sense' is the hallmark of nonsense. Nature does not make sense. Nothing makes sense." 1923: Poet and novelist James Dickey (*Deliverance*) b. Atlanta, Ga.

1874: Gertrude Stein b. Allegheny, Pa. The woman who boasted "I have been the creative literary mind of the century" had her detractors. "What an old covered wagon she is!" F. Scott Fitzgerald remarked of her years later, and Wyndham Lewis likened her prose to "a cold suet-roll of fabulously reptilian length." 1907: James Michener b. New York City. His *Tales from the South Pacific* won the Pulitzer Prize only days after he was advised by an elder at Macmillan to drop writing and stick to editing. 1964: "It wasn't until the Nobel Prize that they really thawed out. They couldn't understand my books, but they could understand $30,000."— William Faulkner on reviewers, in the *National Observer*. 1980: "Hack fiction exploits curiosity without really satisfying it or making connections between it and anything else in the world."—Vincent Canby, in *The New York Times*.

Opposite: Sylvia Beach and James Joyce *Right:* Gertrude Stein and Alice B. Toklas

1900: Jacques Prévert b. Paris. 1988: Isabel Allende (*The House of Spirits* and *Eva Luna*) recollects her newspapering life in Chile before the 1973 coup d'état forced her to flee: "I can't go back to journalism because I was a terrible journalist—I couldn't be objective enough! Now, writing novels is my private orgy. I'm never afraid of the white paper. It is something like a clean sheet recently ironed to make love. It's always a pleasure." 1990: Martin Amis, son of Kingsley Amis, muses on the place of romance in his acid tales of urban blight (*London Fields* and *Time's Arrow*) in Margaret Thatcher's England: "I think there's a lot of romanticism in my work, but it's thwarted by distortion and perversity, false commercial images in TV, literature, porn. The fact is, my satire wouldn't work if what I'm satirizing were not valued. Like Philip Larkin's poetry, love is conspicuous by its absence."

1626: Madame de Sévigné b. Paris. 1914: William Burroughs (*Naked Lunch* and *Junkie*) b. St. Louis, Mo. 1989: Writers Geoffrey Wolff (*Duke of Deception*) and Tobias Wolff (*This Boy's Life*), brothers who grew up on separate coasts after their parents divorced, talk of their ultimate reunion: "Geoffrey was the first person I'd ever met for whom books were the only way in which you could in good conscience spend your life," Tobias declares, and Geoffrey adds, "Most of what we do when we get together now is laugh."

1564: Christopher Marlowe b. Canterbury, England.

1478: Sir Thomas More b. London. 1764: Ann Radcliffe, Gothic novelist, b. London. 1812: Charles Dickens b. Portsmouth, England. Oscar Wilde once quipped, "One must have a heart of stone to read the death of Little Nell by Dickens without laughing." V. S. Pritchett was more ambiguous: "I swallow Dickens whole and put up with the indigestion." 1867: Laura Ingalls Wilder b. Pepin, Wis. 1885: Sinclair Lewis b. Sauk Centre, Minn. He later described himself as a "dull fellow whose virtue—if there is any—is to be found in his books."

1819: John Ruskin b. London. 1828: Jules Verne b. Nantes, France. 1851: Kate Chopin b. St. Louis, Mo. 1911: Elizabeth Bishop b. Worcester, Mass. Orphaned at an early age, Bishop never learned to settle down, living in London, Mexico, San Francisco, Key West, Paris, and Brazil. In 1976, accepting an award, she alluded to her poem "Sandpiper": "Yes, all my life I have lived and behaved very much like that sandpiper—just running along the edges of different countries, 'looking for something.'"

1874: Amy Lowell b. Brookline, Mass. Like George Sand, she enjoyed a good cigar. In 1915, fearing a wartime shortage, she bought 10,000 of her favorite Manila brand. 1923: Brendan Behan b. Dublin. Of drama critics, the ferocious playwright later said, "They're like eunuchs in a harem. They're there every night, they see it done every night, they see how it should be done every night, but they can't do it themselves." 1943: Clare Boothe Luce makes her first speech as Connecticut's first congresswoman and creates a stir when, referring to Vice President Henry Wallace, she says: "Much of what Mr. Wallace calls his global thinking is, no matter how you slice it, still globaloney." 1944: Alice Walker b. Eatonton, Ga. "We will be ourselves and free, or die in the attempt," the author of *The Color Purple* later wrote. "Harriet Tubman was not our great-grandmother for nothing."

Alice Walker

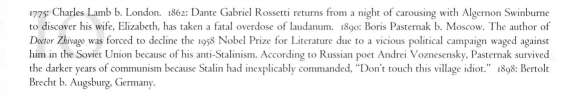

1775: Charles Lamb b. London. 1862: Dante Gabriel Rossetti returns from a night of carousing with Algernon Swinburne to discover his wife, Elizabeth, has taken a fatal overdose of laudanum. 1890: Boris Pasternak b. Moscow. The author of *Doctor Zhivago* was forced to decline the 1958 Nobel Prize for Literature due to a vicious political campaign waged against him in the Soviet Union because of his anti-Stalinism. According to Russian poet Andrei Voznesensky, Pasternak survived the darker years of communism because Stalin had inexplicably commanded, "Don't touch this village idiot." 1898: Bertolt Brecht b. Augsburg, Germany.

1963: Sylvia Plath, 30, commits suicide in London.

1663: Cotton Mather b. Boston. The Puritan insisted that excretory activities be accompanied "with some holy thoughts of a repenting and an abased soul," and formulated prayers to utter "when I am at any time obliged into the urinary discharges." 1809: Charles Darwin b. Shrewsbury, England, on the same day as Abraham Lincoln b. Hodgenville, Ky. 1938: Judy Blume b. Elizabeth, N.J. 1961: "A great pleasure resulting from being rid of servants—one can throw away all the presents they have ever given one."—Evelyn Waugh, in his journal.

Lincoln's Birthday

1903: Georges Simenon b. Lièges, Belgium. "Writing is not a profession, but a vocation of unhappiness," this prolific writer and creator of the astute Inspector Maigret once said. 1959: "Slang is a language that rolls up its sleeves, spits on its hands and goes to work," Carl Sandburg tells *The New York Times*. 1974: Aleksandr Solzhenitsyn is expelled from the Soviet Union. 1990: Seventy-four-year-old Indian writer Khushwant Singh says of his country's new wave of controversial young writers: "This is honest writing. If [the subject matter] is stark poverty, then it's stark poverty, and there's no point in covering it up with mystic humbug." The new Indian "brat pack" includes Shashi Tharoor, Amitav Ghosh, and Anita Desai.

14

1817: Frederick Douglass b. Tuckahoe, Md. 1856: Frank Harris b. County Galway, Ireland. Oscar Wilde quipped about the author of the erotic memoir *My Life and Loves*: "Frank Harris is invited to all the great houses in England—once."

Valentine's Day

15

1986: The original typescript of Henry Miller's *Tropic of Cancer* is sold at Sotheby's for $165,000. 1989: In the wake of Salman Rushdie's *Satanic Verses* being called "hate literature" by the Islamic world, the Ayatollah Khomeini declares the author and publishers of the book "sentenced to death." The decree forces Rushdie into hiding.

16

1838: Henry Adams b. Boston. The author of *The Education of Henry Adams* said of himself, "I want to look like an American Voltaire or Gibbon, but am slowly settling down to be a third-rate Boswell hunting for a Dr. Johnson."

17

1879: Novelist Dorothy Canfield Fisher, chronicler of Vermont life, b. Lawrence, Kans. 1929: Chaim Potok b. New York City. 1957: Paul Engel tells *The New York Times*, "Poetry is ordinary language raised to the Nth power. Poetry is boned with ideas, nerved and blooded with emotions, all held together by the delicate, tough skin of words." 1986: Margaret Atwood responds to some people labeling her best-seller *The Handmaid's Tale* a feminist tract: "Novels are not slogans. If I wanted to say just one thing, I would hire a billboard. If I wanted to say just one thing to one person, I would write a letter. Novels are something else."

1885: Mark Twain's *Huckleberry Finn* is published.   1909: Wallace Stegner b. Lake Mills, Iowa.   1931: Toni Morrison b. Lorain, Ohio. The winner of the 1993 Nobel Prize for Literature once told *The New York Times*: "I really think the range of emotions and perceptions I have had access to as a black person and as a female person are greater than those of people who are neither. . . . So it seems to me that my world did not shrink because I was a black female writer. It just got bigger."

1903: Kay Boyle b. St. Paul, Minn.   1917: Carson McCullers b. Columbus, Ga.   1932: William Faulkner completes work on *Light in August.*

Carson McCullers, 1940

1950: Dylan Thomas arrives in New York City to deliver his first series of American poetry readings. It is in that city that he will drink himself to death, at the White Horse Tavern in Greenwich Village.

1903: Anaïs Nin b. Neuilly, France. Henry Miller said that her notorious but barely published diaries ranked "beside the revelations of Saint Augustine, Petronius, Abélard, Rousseau, Proust." Of him, she wrote in November 1932: "He never writes in cold blood: he is always writing in white heat." 1907: W. H. Auden b. York, England. "He has a face like a wedding cake left out in the rain," it would be said of him. 1925: The first issue of *The New Yorker* is published. Its founder and editor, Harold Ross, claims it will "reflect metropolitan life," and will not be "for the old lady in Dubuque."

Anaïs Nin

Christopher Isherwood and W. H. Auden

1788: Arthur Schopenhauer b. Danzig, Germany. 1892: Edna St. Vincent Millay b. Rockland, Maine. Her middle name came from the New York City hospital where her uncle had been hospitalized. "A person who publishes a book willfully appears before the populace with his pants down," she once said. 1917: Jane Bowles b. New York City. 1990: Dame Iris Murdoch, reminiscing about her years in Paris with Jean-Paul Sartre, declares: "I wish that more English people would have an easy day-to-day rapport with the French. . . . They admire Stendhal and Flaubert, but they don't feel close to them, the way they do to the Russians. Tolstoy and Dostoyevsky *are* English, they think. They even think that Proust is English, too."

Washington's Birthday

Edna St. Vincent Millay

1633: Samuel Pepys b. London. 1868: W. E. B. DuBois b. Great Barrington, Mass.

1786: Wilhelm Grimm b. Hanau, Germany. 1852: George Moore b. Ballyglass, County Mayo, Ireland. Oscar Wilde would one day snipe: "Know him? I know him so well that I haven't spoken to him in ten years."

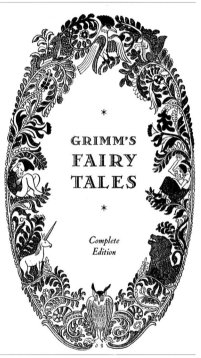

1917: Anthony Burgess b. Manchester, England. "The adult relation to books," he once remarked, "is one of absorbing rather than being absorbed."

Title page for *Grimm's Fairy Tales*

1802: Victor Hugo b. Besançon, France. When he wrote, he gave all his clothes to his servant with orders that they be returned only after several hours, when he had finished his day's work. When he wanted to know how his publishers liked *Les Misérables*, he wrote them a succinct: "?" They promptly responded: "!" **1956:** At a party in Cambridge, England, Sylvia Plath, then a Fulbright scholar, meets Ted Hughes and writes of him: "The one man in the room who was as big as his poems, huge . . . I screamed in myself, thinking: oh, to give myself crashing, fighting, to you."

1807: Henry Wadsworth Longfellow b. Portland, Me. **1902:** John Steinbeck b. Salinas, Calif. He later said: "Writers are a little below clowns and a little above trained seals." **1986:** Robert Penn Warren is appointed the first U.S. poet laureate. "I don't expect you'll hear me writing any poems to the greater glory of Ronald and Nancy Reagan," he declares.

1533: Montaigne b. Périgueux, France. He once said he would rather see his children burned than his books. **1909:** Stephen Spender b. London. "Great poetry is always written by somebody straining to go beyond what he can do," he said. **1988:** Fay Weldon declares that the golden age of literature in England is not dead: "We are not denatured remnants of the human race. On the contrary, we are more sensitive, more humane, more culturally aware than our forefathers. We understand better than ever what it feels like to be someone else. We are avid, avid readers."

46 B.C.: Julius Caesar is said to have adjusted this year by fixing 365 days and six hours as the length of a year, with one day intercalated every four years—a leap. **1228:** A law passed in Scotland allows women to propose marriage only in leap year.

Leap Year

Lithograph by Thomas Hart Benton for John Steinbeck's *Grapes of Wrath*

MARCH

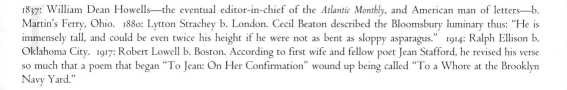

1837: William Dean Howells—the eventual editor-in-chief of the *Atlantic Monthly*, and American man of letters—b. Martin's Ferry, Ohio. **1880:** Lytton Strachey b. London. Cecil Beaton described the Bloomsbury luminary thus: "He is immensely tall, and could be even twice his height if he were not as bent as sloppy asparagus." **1914:** Ralph Ellison b. Oklahoma City. **1917:** Robert Lowell b. Boston. According to first wife and fellow poet Jean Stafford, he revised his verse so much that a poem that began "To Jean: On Her Confirmation" wound up being called "To a Whore at the Brooklyn Navy Yard."

1859: Sholem Aleichem b. Kiev, Russia. The Russian-born Yiddish author was called "The Jewish Mark Twain," but when he met his namesake in New York City, Twain deferred: "I am the American *Sholem Aleichem*." **1883:** In response to criticism about the lack of meter in his poetry, H. G. Wells exclaims, "Meters are used for gas, not the outpourings of the human heart." **1904:** Theodor Seuss Geisel (Dr. Seuss) b. Springfield, Mass. He remarked in 1986, "You can get help from teachers, but you are going to have to learn a lot by yourself, sitting alone in a room." **1942:** John Irving b. Exeter, N. H. He claimed the ministers of his youth as an early influence: "They seemed intelligent, compassionate, kind. They were articulate. . . .They were among my first contacts with seizing someone's attention, telling a story, and persuading you, emotionally and psychologically, to believe something."

1922: F. Scott Fitzgerald's *Beautiful and Damned* is published. **1985:** "The more I like a book, the more slowly I read," Anatole Broyard writes in *The New York Times*. "This spontaneous talking back to a book [is] one of the things that makes reading so valuable."

1848: George Sand and Frédéric Chopin meet for the last time.

1839: Charlotte Brontë declines a marriage proposal, writing: "I am not the serious, grave, cool-hearted individual you suppose; you would think me romantic and eccentric." 1853: Howard Pyle b. Wilmington, Del. 1870: Frank Norris b. Chicago. The author of *The Octopus* (1901) asserted: "I never took off the hat to fashion and held it out for pennies. By God, I told them the truth."

1806: Elizabeth Barrett (later Browning) b. Durham, England. On this day in 1832, she enters in her journal, "My birthday! In another year, where shall I be— & what shall I have suffered?—A great deal I dare say—and my heart appears to be giving way even now." 1885: Ring Lardner b. Niles, Mich. He worked as a meter reader before he got a post at the *Chicago Tribune* in 1913. "When I entered a cellar and saw a rat reading the meter ahead of me," he later recalled, "I accepted his reading and went on to the next house." 1928: Gabriel García Márquez b. Colombia. As John Steinbeck did, he directs his writing to a single person—preferably a friend—and writes just to him or her. 1966: Literary critic Lionel Trilling tells *The New York Times*, "Youth is a time when we find the book we give up but do not get over."

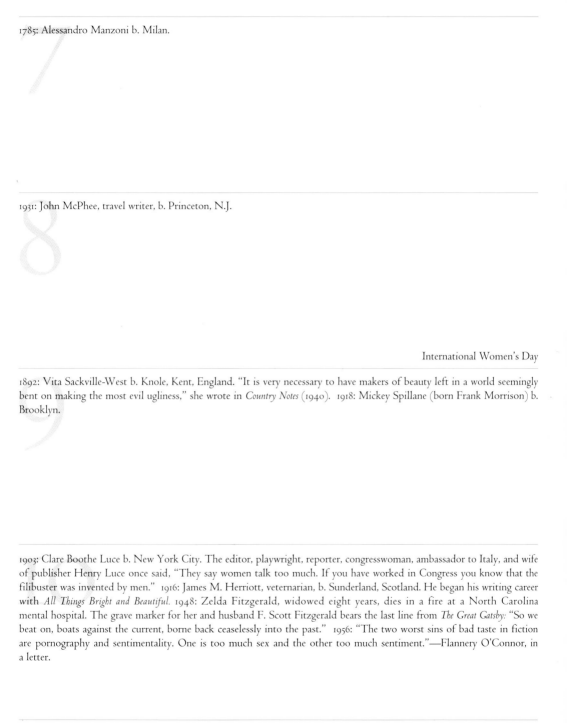

1785: Alessandro Manzoni b. Milan.

1931: John McPhee, travel writer, b. Princeton, N.J.

International Women's Day

1892: Vita Sackville-West b. Knole, Kent, England. "It is very necessary to have makers of beauty left in a world seemingly bent on making the most evil ugliness," she wrote in *Country Notes* (1940). **1918:** Mickey Spillane (born Frank Morrison) b. Brooklyn.

1903: Clare Boothe Luce b. New York City. The editor, playwright, reporter, congresswoman, ambassador to Italy, and wife of publisher Henry Luce once said, "They say women talk too much. If you have worked in Congress you know that the filibuster was invented by men." **1916:** James M. Herriott, veternarian, b. Sunderland, Scotland. He began his writing career with *All Things Bright and Beautiful.* **1948:** Zelda Fitzgerald, widowed eight years, dies in a fire at a North Carolina mental hospital. The grave marker for her and husband F. Scott Fitzgerald bears the last line from *The Great Gatsby:* "So we beat on, boats against the current, borne back ceaselessly into the past." **1956:** "The two worst sins of bad taste in fiction are pornography and sentimentality. One is too much sex and the other too much sentiment."—Flannery O'Connor, in a letter.

1818: *Frankenstein* by Mary Shelley is published.

1846: Elizabeth Barrett writes to Robert Browning: "If it will satisfy you that I should know you, love you, love you—when then indeed . . . You should have my soul to stand on if it could make you stand higher."   1863: Gabriele D'Annunzio b. Pescara, Italy. The Italian poet claimed that more than a thousand husbands hated him, and that his pillows were filled with locks of hair from the women he had seduced.   1922: Jack Kerouac b. Lowell, Mass. In 1960, he told the *New York Journal American,* "It is not my fault that certain so-called bohemian elements have found in my writings something to hang their peculiar beatnik theories on."   1928: Edward Albee b. Washington, D.C.

1892: Janet Flanner b. Boston. The Paris correspondent to *The New Yorker* for some fifty years once wrote: "By jove, no wonder women don't love war nor understand it, nor can operate in it as a rule; it takes a man to suffer what other men have invented. . . . Women have invented nothing in all that, except the men who were born as male babies and grew up to be men big enough to be killed fighting."

1826: Sir Walter Scott writes of Jane Austen in his journal: "She has a talent for describing the involvements and characters of ordinary life which is to me the most wonderful I have ever met with. The Big Bow-Wow strain I can do myself, but the exquisite touch . . . is denied to me." 1850: Honoré de Balzac, 51, marries Polish countess Evelina Hanska, after eighteen years of romantic correspondence. 1887: Sylvia Beach, who will found the renowned Shakespeare & Company bookstore in Paris, is born in her father's parsonage in Baltimore, Md.

1963: Robert Frost tells *Vogue*: "Talking is a hydrant in the yard and writing is a faucet in the house. Opening the first takes pressure off the second."

Robert Frost

1839: René-François-Armand Sully-Prudhomme, the first writer to be awarded the Nobel Prize for Literature, in 1901, b. Paris. 1850: *The Scarlet Letter* by Nathaniel Hawthorne is published.

1846: Kate Greenaway (*Mother Goose*) b. London. 1985: Jayne Anne Phillips philosophizes to *The New York Times* about writing a second novel: "As before, there is a great silence, with no end in sight. The writer surrenders, listening." 1992: "Politics disappears; it vanishes. What remains constant is human life," declares Russian writer Tatyana Tolstaya (*On the Golden Porch*), great-grandniece of Leo Tolstoy. "So I try to develop a perspective in my writing where politics is just one of the pieces of furniture in this furnished world. It is not the purpose. It is not the goal."

Saint Patrick's Day

John Updike

1842: Stéphane Mallarmé b. Paris. "The world exists to be put in a book," he once said. 1893: Wilfred Owen b. Shropshire, England. 1932: John Updike b. Shillington, Pa. He once commented, "Writers take their words seriously—perhaps the last professional class that does—and they struggle to steer their own through the crosswinds of meddling editors and careless typesetters and obtuse and malevolent reviewers into the lap of the ideal reader."

1821: Sir Richard F. Burton, English explorer and translator of the *Arabian Nights* and the *Kama Sutra,* b. Torquay, Devonshire, England. At his death in 1890, his wife, who believed his work to be obscene, burned all his unpublished manuscripts. 1933: Philip Roth b. Newark, N.J. He once said, "The best readers come to fiction to be free of all that isn't fiction."

43 B.C.: Ovid b. Sulmona in the Arbruzzi. He is banished from Rome by Augustus in A.D. 8, for writing *The Art of Love,* a lovemaking manual. 1828: Henrik Ibsen b. Skien, Norway. When a friend once asked the playwright why he had a picture of Strindberg over his desk, he replied, "He is my mortal enemy and shall hang there and watch while I write."

Henrik Ibsen

1905: Phyllis McGinley b. Ontario, Ore. "Sin . . . has been made not only ugly but passé. People are no longer sinful, they are only immature or underprivileged or frightened or, more particularly, sick," she later wrote in "In Defense of Sin."

1958: "The poem . . . is a little myth of man's capacity of making life meaningful," Robert Penn Warren tells the *Saturday Review*. "And in the end, the poem is not a thing we see—it is, rather, a light by which we may see—and what we see is life." 1987: "[Tuberculosis was] the best disease I ever had. If I hadn't had it, I might be a second-rate shrink practicing in Birmingham, at best," Walker Percy, in *The New York Times*, on the convalescence that turned his interest from psychiatry to writing.

1900: Erich Fromm b. Frankfurt-am-Main, Germany. 1913: Jack London sends letters to Winston Churchill, H. G. Wells, and George Bernard Shaw, asking all three writers how much they are paid for "their stuff." 1917: Virginia and Leonard Woolf buy a small handpress and start the Hogarth Press in their dining room, later publishing T. S. Eliot, Maxim Gorky, Katherine Mansfield, and E. M. Forster.

1905: Jules Verne, 77, dies in Amiens, France. 1919: Lawrence Ferlinghetti b. Yonkers. 1957: In his acceptance speech for the National Book Award, Richard Wilbur says, "It is true that the poet does not directly address his neighbors; but he does address a great congress of persons who dwell at the back of his mind, a congress of all those who have taught him and whom he has admired; they constitute his ideal audience and his better self." 1986: Of poetry, John Updike tells *The New York Times*, "There's a crystallization that goes on in a poem which the young man can bring off, but which the middle-aged man can't."

1811: Percy Bysshe Shelley is expelled from Oxford for denying he wrote *The Necessity of Atheism.* 1820: Anne Brontë b. Yorkshire, England. In 1847's *Agnes Grey*, the youngest Brontë sister wrote: "All true histories contain instruction; though, in some, the treasure may be hard to find, and when found, so trivial in quantity, that the dry, shrivelled kernel scarcely compensates for the trouble of cracking the nut." 1925: Flannery O'Connor b. Savannah, Ga. The Southern writer and devout Catholic once wrote, "I don't deserve any credit for turning the other cheek, as my tongue is always in it." 1980: "It's a nervous work," Shirley Hazzard says to *The New York Times* of writing. "The state that you need to write is the state that others are paying large sums to get rid of."

Anne Brontë

1859: A. E. Housman b. Worcestershire, England. He later said, "Great literature should do some good to the reader; must quicken his perception though dull, and sharpen his discrimination though blunt, and mellow the rawness of his personal opinions." 1874: Robert Frost b. San Francisco. The poet, who won the Pulitzer Prize in 1921, 1924, 1937, and 1943, once said, "Poets are like baseball pitchers. Both have their moments. The intervals are the tough things." 1897: Mrs. Oscar Wilde writes her brother about her husband's imprisonment for his affair with Lord Alfred Douglas: "I think his fate is rather like Humpty Dumpty's, quite as tragic and quite as impossible to put right." 1930: "I never foresaw that writing for the Press would be actually so degrading. What I dread is that I might get to like it."—Sir Harold Nicolson, in his journal. 1990: "I write about love, yes, but not about tenderness," the 75-year-old Marguerite Duras confesses. "I don't like tender people. I myself am very harsh. When I love someone, I desire them. But tenderness supposes the exclusion of desire."

1923: Shusako Endo b. Tokyo. 1931: Arnold Bennett dies of typhoid at 64.

1868: Aleksei Maksimovich Pyeshkov (pseudonym Maxim Gorky) b. Novgorod, Russia. His nom de plume means "the bitter." 1909: Nelson Algren b. Detroit, Mich. 1936: Mario Vargas Llosa b. Peru. He once said, "If you are killed because you are a writer, that's the maximum expression of respect, you know." 1941: J. D. Salinger, working as an entertainer on a Swedish cruise liner, sells his first Holden Caulfield story to *The New Yorker* and begins a five-year wait for its publication. 1941: Virginia Woolf, 59, ends her life by walking into the River Ouse, in North Yorkshire.

1952: "Whether children will find anything amusing in it, only time will tell."—E. B. White writes to his editor, about *Charlotte's Web.*

1844: Paul Verlaine b. Metz, France. After an argument with his lover, the poet Arthur Rimbaud, he shot and wounded the younger poet; Verlaine then spent the next ten years in jail and became a Catholic. 1880: Sean O'Casey b. Dublin. 1981: "I think women dwell quite a bit on the duress under which they work . . . " Toni Morrison tells *Newsweek*. "We are traditionally rather proud of ourselves for having slipped creative work in there between the domestic chores and obligations. I'm not sure we deserve such big A-pluses for all that."

1621: Andrew Marvell b. Winestead, England. 1809: Nikolai Gogol b. Sorochinsk, Russia. Gogol *twice* burned the second part of his *Dead Souls* (1842) manuscript—once during a spiritual crisis, and again, seven years later, at the urging of a priest who encouraged him to renounce literature. 1914: Octavio Paz b. Mixcoac, Mexico. "There can be a 'boom' in petroleum or wheat," he said, "but there can't be a boom in the novel and less still in poetry." 1926: John Fowles b. Leigh-on-Sea, England.

Illustration by Garth Williams for *Charlotte's Web*

APRIL

1929: Milan Kundera b. Brno, Czechoslovakia. In *Comedy Is Everywhere* he wrote, "Ideology wants to convince you that its truth is absolute. A novel shows you that everything is relative." 1957: Rod Serling tells *Vogue*, "Every writer is a frustrated actor who recites his lines in the hidden auditorium of his skull."

1725: Giovanni Jacopo Casanova (*Memoirs*) b. Venice. 1805: Hans Christian Andersen b. Odense, Denmark. "Most of the people who will walk after me will be children," he instructed the composer who was writing his funeral march, "so make the beat keep time with little steps." 1836: Charles Dickens and Catherine Hogarth are married. They will have ten children and separate in 1858. 1840: Emile Zola b. Paris.

1783: Washington Irving b. New York City. Charles Dickens will one day write, "I don't go upstairs to bed two nights out of seven without taking Washington Irving under my arm." 1920: F. Scott Fitzgerald and Zelda Sayre marry four days after the publication of *This Side of Paradise*. 1990: On the publication of *The Things They Carried*, a collection of short stories inspired by his experiences in the Vietnam war, Tim O'Brien remarks: "Storytelling is the essential human activity. The harder the situation, the more essential it is. . . . I would be mad not to tell the stories I know."

1914: Marguerite Duras b. Indochina. The author of *The Lover* would later call writing "a matter of deciphering something already there, something you've already done in the sleep of your life, in its organic rumination, unbeknown to you. Writing isn't just telling stories. . . . It's the telling of a story, and the absence of a story. It's telling a story through its absence." 1928: Maya Angelou b. St. Louis, Mo. "The fact that the adult American Negro female emerges a formidable character is often met with amazement, distaste and even belligerence," she wrote in 1969's *I Know Why the Caged Bird Sings*. "It is seldom accepted as the inevitable outcome of the struggle won by survivors, and deserves respect if not enthusiastic acceptance."

Opposite: Maya Angelou *Above:* Emile Zola

1837: Algernon Swinburne b. London. "He had the finest ear, perhaps, of any English poet," W. H. Auden said of him. 1947: *Publishers Weekly* reports that negotiations between Evelyn Waugh and MGM for a *Brideshead Revisited* screenplay fall through, thirty-four years before the story's hugely successful public television adaptation puts Waugh's book on the best-seller list. 1987: "The area of Paris where we've located is on the Left Bank. Many bookstores nearby. Ray goes into one to see if they have his book. They don't. At the Café Bonaparte I say: 'Well, it doesn't look like you're going to be mobbed here.' Ray: 'Well, it's only Sunday.'"—Tess Gallagher, poet and wife of Raymond Carver, in her journal.

1327: In the Church of St. Clara at Avignon, Petrarch sees for the first time the real-life "Laura" who would inspire 366 love poems. 1866: Lincoln Steffens b. San Francisco.

1770: William Wordsworth b. Cockermouth, Cumberland, England. 1931: Donald Barthelme b. Philadelphia. 1949: *South Pacific*, based on James Michener's collection of short stories inspired by his experiences as a naval historian in New Guinea and Tahiti, opens on Broadway and subsequently runs for 1,925 performances. 1987: "If [my wife] doesn't like something I've done, I won't submit it to my publisher, but neither will I take her out to dinner, come home with flowers, or even water the vegetable garden."—Mordecai Richler, in his journal.

1986: In *The New York Times*, William Carlos Williams says, "When they ask me, as of late they frequently do, how I have for so many years continued an equal interest in medicine and poetry, I reply that they amount for me to nearly the same thing."

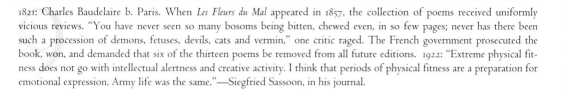

1821: Charles Baudelaire b. Paris. When *Les Fleurs du Mal* appeared in 1857, the collection of poems received uniformly vicious reviews. "You have never seen so many bosoms being bitten, chewed even, in so few pages; never has there been such a procession of demons, fetuses, devils, cats and vermin," one critic raged. The French government prosecuted the book, won, and demanded that six of the thirteen poems be removed from all future editions. 1922: "Extreme physical fitness does not go with intellectual alertness and creative activity. I think that periods of physical fitness are a preparation for emotional expression. Army life was the same."—Siegfried Sassoon, in his journal.

1941: Paul Theroux b. Medford, Mass. He once said, "Fiction gives us a second chance that life denies us." 1988: Gabriel García Márquez explains why he will not permit a film version of *One Hundred Years of Solitude*: "It [the book] will be destroyed, because film does not allow for people to feel it is about something or someone they know. The face of the actor, of Gregory Peck, becomes the face of the character. It cannot be your uncle, unless your uncle looks like Gregory Peck." 1988: On the publication of *The Sportswriter*, Richard Ford muses: "People say all sorts of things to you about making it as a writer. But there's no it to make. There's no gradient, no stepladder. I've just given everything I've ever written my very best—my absolute, greatest best shot. . . . Now they like me. Next year, who knows what they'll do?"

1914: George Bernard Shaw's *Pygmalion* opens at His Majesty's Theatre in London with Herbert Beerbohm Tree as Higgins and Mrs. Patrick Campbell as Eliza; it is the eve of Shaw's fifteenth anniversary of corresponding with the actress. 1931: Dorothy Parker concludes what she called a ten-year "reign of terror" as drama critic for *The New Yorker*.

1709: The first issue of *The Tatler* is published.

1906: Samuel Beckett b. Dublin. On his eightieth birthday, he told *The New York Times*: "I write about myself with the pencil and in the same exercise book as about him. It is no longer I, but another whose life is just beginning." 1909: Eudora Welty b. Jackson, Miss. Carolyn Heilbrun wrote of Welty's *One Writer's Beginnings*, "There can be no question that to have written a truthful autobiography would have defied every one of her instincts for loyalty and privacy. . . . What then do I want from her? Would life not be preferable if we were all like Eudora Welty? It would." 1991: "I'm very interested in what's going on inside of people's heads. Because our surface is no guide at all . . . " Josephine Hart declares on the publication of *Damage.* "There are, I think, in all of us, all sorts of things going on all the time, from ideas of terrible destruction to feelings of intense joy. Which we cover up. And I'm very interested in that."

1889: Arnold Toynbee b. London. 1963: André Maurois tells *The New York Times*, "In literature as in love, we are astonished at what is chosen by others." 1988: Ariel Dorfman, fifteen years after being barred from Chile in the wake of a military coup, says: "Words become a way of returning to your country—a cemetery, but also a resurrection ground." 1991: Israeli writer Amos Oz (*Where the Jackals Howl and Other Stories* and *To Know a Woman*) remarks: "I find that my characters often believe in something I myself do not believe . . . such as happiness, love, total compassion, forgiveness, redemption. I share these totalizing impulses, but they are well under control."

1802: Returning from Eusemere, on one of their legendary walks, Dorothy Wordsworth points out to brother William what she later records in her journal as "a few daffodils close to the water-side." Her brother's account, in the poem "I Wandered Lonely as a Cloud" (1807): "Ten thousand saw I at a glance,/Tossing their heads in sprightly dance." 1843: Henry James b. New York City. When Edith Wharton wrote him that she would buy an automobile with the profits of her last novel, James replied: "With the proceeds of my last novel I purchased a small go-cart, or hand-barrow, on which my guests' luggage is wheeled from the station to my house. It needs a coat of paint. With the proceeds of my next novel I shall have it painted." 1977: "My editor told me that the second half of the book needed a damn good love scene, and there is nothing I dislike writing more. . . . You can only say 'he stuck it in her' so many ways."—Colleen McCullough, on her best-seller *The Thorn Birds*, in the *Guardian.* 1978: "A book is like a piece of rope; it takes on meaning only in connection with the things it holds together."—Norman Cousins, in the *Saturday Review.*

1787: Royall Tyler's *The Contrast,* the first professionally produced American comedy, appears at New York City's John Street Theater. 1844: Anatole France b. Paris. The writer of *Crainquebille* (1904) once said, "There are no bad books any more than there are ugly women." 1922: Kingsley Amis b. London.

1839: "If you cannot grow plump and rosy and tough and vigorous without being changed into another nature, then I do think for this short life, you had better remain just what you are."—Nathaniel Hawthorne in a love letter to his ailing wife, Sophia. 1883: Karen Blixen (Isak Dinesen) b. Rungsted, Denmark. 1897: Thornton Wilder b. Madison, Wis. He once said, "I think I write in order to discover on my shelf a new book which I would enjoy reading, or to see a new play that would engross me." 1928: Cynthia Ozick b. New York City. In *The First Ms. Reader* of 1972, she wrote, "Moral: In saying what is obvious, never choose cunning. Yelling is better."

© JILL KREMENTZ

Eudora Welty

1958: After thirteen years in custody a U.S. federal court concludes that Ezra Pound is incurably insane and can no longer be held under indictment for treason. Upon his release in 1958 from St. Elizabeth's Hospital he reflects: "How did it go in the madhouse? Rather badly. But what other place could one live in America?"

1928: *The Oxford English Dictionary* is completed.   1992: "There's no such thing as life without bloodshed," asserts Cormac McCarthy amid the success of his novel *All the Pretty Horses*. "I think the notion that the species can be improved in some way, that everyone could live in harmony, is a really dangerous idea. Those who are afflicted with this notion are the first ones to give up their souls, their freedom. Your desire that it be that way will enslave you and make your life vacuous."

1925: "Happiness is to have a little string onto which things will attach themselves . . . as if dipped loosely into a wave of treasure it brings up pearls sticking to it."—Virginia Woolf, in her journal.

21 1816: Charlotte Brontë b. Thornton, Yorkshire, England. She wrote to her publisher that she was "neither man nor woman," and went on to say, "I come before you as an author only. It is the sole standard by which you have a right to judge me—the sole ground on which I accept your judgment." 1910: Mark Twain, 75, dies of angina pectoris in Redding, Conn., coinciding with the reappearance of Halley's Comet, which had last shone in the year he was born. 1939: Ezra Pound arrives in New York after thirty years abroad and accepts an honorary degree from his alma mater, Hamilton College.

22 1707: Henry Fielding b. Glastonbury, England. 1766: Germaine Necker (Madame de Staël) b. Paris. The French woman of letters and legendary salon-keeper once said, "The phantom of ennui forever pursues me."

23 1564: William Shakespeare b. Stratford-on-Avon. 1616: William Shakespeare and Miguel de Cervantes die on the same day. 1899: Vladimir Nabokov b. St. Petersburg, Russia. He once proclaimed, "Style and structure are the essence of a book; great ideas are hogwash." 1985: In the wake of the success of her *One Writer's Beginnings*, Eudora Welty speaks to a group of young writers at New York City's 92nd Street Y. She provides technical points but insists, "Of course, that is not the same as making you into a writer. That comes from inside, and is in the lap of the gods."

24

1815: Anthony Trollope b. London. 1905: Robert Penn Warren b. Guthrie, Ky. He once told the *National Observer*, "I've been to a lot of places and done a lot of things, but writing was always first. It's a kind of pain I can't do without."

25

1826: Lord Byron leaves England forever for exile in Europe. 1873: Walter de la Mare b. Charlton, Kent, England. On his deathbed, when his youngest daughter asked if fruit or flowers might improve his condition, the poet responded: "No, no, my dear. Too late for fruit, too soon for flowers." 1989: On the publication of *A Prayer for Owen Meany*, John Irving says: "I would like to be judged by how well I set up the shop. I have a very simple formula . . . you've got to be more interested on page 320 than on page 32."

26

1731: Daniel Defoe dies in London, hiding from creditors. 1893: Anita Loos b. Mount Shasta, Calif. She wrote in 1974's *Kiss Hollywood Goodbye*, "It's true that the French have a certain obsession with sex, but it's a particularly adult obsession . . . to a Frenchman sex provides the most economical way to have fun. The French are a logical race." 1914: Bernard Malamud b. Brooklyn. "The idea is to get the pencil moving quickly," he said of writing. "Once you've got some words looking back at you, you can take two or three—or throw them away and look for others." 1932: Returning to New York from Mexico on a Guggenheim Fellowship, 34-year-old Hart Crane takes a fatal leap into the Caribbean Sea from the stern of the S.S. *Orizaba*, calling "Goodbye, everybody!"

THE

L I F E

AND

STRANGE SURPRIZING

ADVENTURES

OF

ROBINSON CRUSOE,

Of *YORK*, MARINER:

Who lived Eight and Twenty Years,
all alone in an un-inhabited Iſland on the
Coaſt of AMERICA, near the Mouth of
the Great River of OROONOQUE;

Having been caſt on Shore by Shipwreck, where-
In all the Men periſhed but himſelf.

WITH

An Account how he was at laſt as ſtrangely deliver'd by PYRATES.

Written by Himſelf.

L O N D O N:
Printed for W. TAYLOR at the *Ship* in *Pater-Noſter-
Row.* MDCCXIX.

Title page for Daniel Defoe's *Robinson Crusoe*

1759: Mary Wollstonecraft b. London. The influential early feminist and mother of writer Mary Shelley would write in a letter: "Society fatigues me inexpressibly. So much so, that finding fault with everyone, I have only reason enough to discover that the fault is in myself." 1961: In a speech at Scripps College, Catherine Drinker Bowen proclaims, "Great artists treasure their time with a bitter and snarling miserliness."

1926: Harper Lee b. Monroeville, Ala. On why she did her best thinking while golfing, the author of *To Kill a Mockingbird* once said, "Well, if [Southern people] know you're working at home they think nothing of walking right in for coffee. But they wouldn't dream of interrupting you at golf." 1962: "Poetry lies its way to the truth," John Ciardi tells the *Saturday Review*. 1986: Of Judith Krantz's *I'll Take Manhattan, Time* magazine says: "In any Krantz work, the good get loved and that is what makes it romantic. The bad get punished, and that is what makes it fiction."

1990: Kazuo Ishiguro discusses the "perfect English butler" at the center of his acclaimed novel *The Remains of the Day:* "I think one of the dangers of having a kind of alter ego in fiction is that you drag in all kinds of things that are irrelevant in an artistic sense simply because they are things that you are concerned with as a person yourself."

1844: During a fishing trip near Concord, Mass., Henry David Thoreau accidentally sets the woods on fire, burning 300 acres. 1877: Alice B. Toklas b. San Francisco. 1945: Annie Dillard b. Pittsburgh, Pa. "Why are we reading, if not in hope that the writer will magnify and dramatize our days," she once wrote, "will illuminate and inspire us with wisdom, courage and the hope of meaningfulness, and press upon our minds the deepest mysteries, so we may feel again their majesty and power?" 1990: "I think there's a great deal of interest in poetry these days," declares Gwendolyn Brooks, poet laureate of Illinois. "Even when people don't label it 'poetry.' What do you think rap is? It's hardly the poetry of the parlor: it's the poetry of the streets. I've wondered if I could write a rap song."

MAY

1841: Edgar Allan Poe publishes a solution to the murder in Dickens's serialized *Barnaby Rudge* in *The Saturday Evening Post.* Dickens later concedes that Poe had figured out the ending before he, Dickens, had ever written it. **1923:** Joseph Heller b. Brooklyn. **1940:** Bobbie Ann Mason b. Mayfield, Ky.

1945: At 72, Colette becomes the first female member of the Académie Goncourt.

1912: D. H. Lawrence and Mrs. Frieda von Richthofen Weekley travel to Metz, Germany, where he is mistakenly arrested as a spy. **1912:** May Sarton b. Belgium. In 1961's *Small Room,* she wrote, "Learning is such a very painful business. It requires humility from people at an age where the natural habitat is arrogance."

1940: James Joyce's wife Nora says to him: "Well, Jim, I haven't read any of your books but I'll have to someday because they must be good considering how well they sell." **1948:** *The Naked and the Dead,* Norman Mailer's first novel, is published.

Charles Dickens

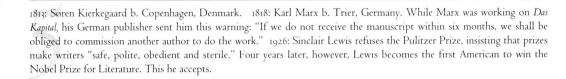

1813: Søren Kierkegaard b. Copenhagen, Denmark.   1818: Karl Marx b. Trier, Germany. While Marx was working on *Das Kapital*, his German publisher sent him this warning: "If we do not receive the manuscript within six months, we shall be obliged to commission another author to do the work."   1926: Sinclair Lewis refuses the Pulitzer Prize, insisting that prizes make writers "safe, polite, obedient and sterile." Four years later, however, Lewis becomes the first American to win the Nobel Prize for Literature. This he accepts.

1861: Indian author and poet Rabindranath Tagore (*Sadhana, The Realization of Life,* and *Gitanjali*) b. Calcutta.   1914: Randall Jarrell b. Nashville, Tenn.   1939: Margaret Drabble b. Sheffield, England. In *The Realms of Gold,* she wrote, "The human mind can bear plenty of reality but not too much unintermittent gloom."   1992: "The transcripts are the ore," explains interviewer Studs Terkel. "I've got to get to the gold dust. It's got to be the person's truth, highlighted. It's not just putting down what people say."

1812: Robert Browning b. London.   1892: Archibald MacLeish b. Glencoe, Ill. "A real writer learns from earlier writers the way a boy learns from an apple orchard . . . by stealing what he has a taste for and can carry off," he once commented.   1989: Wendy Wasserstein, Ntozake Shange, Tina Howe, and Cindy Lou Johnson convene to discuss the status of women playwrights. Shange (*For Colored Girls Who Have Considered Suicide/When the Rainbow Is Enuf*) remarks: "When we go out of this building . . . any of these guys unloading trucks don't see playwrights. They see—they may not even see—a woman. They might see an expletive."

1895: Edmund Wilson b. Red Bank, N. J. His infamous postcard read, in part: "Edmund Wilson regrets that it is impossible for him to: Read manuscripts, write articles or books to order, write forewords or introductions . . . supply personal information about himself, supply opinions on literary or other subjects . . . "   1937: Thomas Pynchon b. Glen Cove, N. Y.

9 1860: James M. Barrie b. Kirriemuir, Scotland. When *Auld Licht Idylls* was published in 1888, he wrote: "For several days after my first book was published I carried it about in my pocket, and took surreptitious peeps at it to make sure the ink had not faded."

10 1898: Historian Ariel Durant (née Ada Kaufman), who will coauthor part of the Story of Civilization series with husband Will, is born in Proskurov, Ukraine. 1932: William Faulkner leaves for Hollywood to write for MGM.

Robert Browning

1927: Six days after the publication of *To the Lighthouse,* Virginia Woolf writes: "What is the use of saying one is indifferent to reviews when positive praise, though mingled with blame, gives one such a start on, that instead of feeling dried up, one feels . . . flooded with ideas?"

Dante Gabriel Rossetti

1828: Dante Gabriel Rossetti b. London. After his young wife took her own life, he laid copies of his poetry in her arms before she was buried. He later regretted the gesture; he secured permission to dig up the coffin and retrieve the poetry, and, in 1870, *Poems* was published to immediate acclaim. 1921: Farley Mowat b. Belleville, Ontario, Canada. 1985: David Leavitt reflects on himself, Peter Cameron, Amy Hempel, and other post–baby boom short-story writers who constitute a new "Lost Generation"—"The short story is the form most appropriate to the age of shortened attention spans, fractured marriages and splintering families in which they grew up."

1907: Daphne du Maurier b. London. 1916: Sholem Aleichem, who feared the number thirteen and never included a page thirteen in his manuscript, dies on his feared day at 63. The date on his tombstone in Glendale, N.Y. reads "May 12a, 1916." 1985: Cleanth Brooks says of Robert Frost in the *Christian Science Monitor,* "The cunning old codger knows that no emphasis often constitutes the most powerful emphasis of all."

1265: Dante Aligheri b. Florence. Although he dedicated *The Divine Comedy* to Beatrice—"the first delight of my soul"—he actually saw her for only three brief moments in his lifetime. Beatrice married and died at 25, unaware that she was a part-ner in one of the world's great literary love stories. 1956: "I specialize in murders of quiet, domestic interest."—Agatha Christie, in *Life* magazine. 1960: Salvatore Quasimodo tells *The New York Times,* "Poetry is the revelation of a feeling that the poet believes to be interior and personal [but] which the reader recognizes as his own."

Dante Aligheri

1856: L. Frank Baum (*The Wonderful Wizard of Oz*) b. Chittenango, N.Y. 1890: Katherine Anne Porter b. Indian Creek, Tex. Of *Ship of Fools*, she said, "I finished the thing, but I think I sprained my soul. I spent 15 years wandering about, weighed horribly with masses of paper and little else. Yet for this vocation of writing I was and am willing to die, and I consider very few other things of the slightest importance." 1904: Clifton Fadiman b. Brooklyn. 1988: Kentucky-born-and-bred Bobbie Ann Mason speaks on behalf of the just-folks folks in her works, *Shiloh and Other Stores* and *In Country:* "The characters in my world don't have the guidance or perspective to know that there might be this *other* view of television or malls . . . I don't judge them for it. When they go to the shopping mall, and many of them go just to window shop, they're looking at deliverance from a hard way of life."

1836: Edgar Allan Poe marries his tubercular cousin, Virginia Clemm. 1912: Studs Terkel b. New York City. 1929: Adrienne Rich b. Baltimore, Md. This poet and author of *Of Woman Born* would say that "those who speak largely of the human condition are usually those most exempt from its oppressions—whether of sex, race or servitude."

1882: Dorothy Richardson b. Abingdon, Oxfordshire, England. In *Pilgrimage*, she wrote, "It will all go on as long as women are stupid enough to go on bringing men into the world . . . " 1928: Evelyn Waugh writes to *The Times Literary Supplement* (London), complaining that in a review of one of his books, he was referred to throughout as "Miss Waugh." 1974: "Life has confirmed for me the thoughts and impressions I had when I was 18, as if it was all intuition."—Françoise Sagan, in *W* magazine.

1824: "A small signal at the window . . . a half-closed shutter or a half-lowered blind, would tell me that I could come up. If I do not see this sign that you are alone I shall refrain from knocking on the door and will try again a quarter of an hour later."—Stendhal, in a love letter to Madame Curial. 1872: Bertrand Russell b. Trelleck, Wales. "Anyone who hopes that in time it may be possible to abolish war should give serious thought to the problem of satisfying harmlessly the instincts that we inherit from long generations of savages," he later remarked. "For my part I find a sufficient outlet in detective stories, where I alternately identify myself with the murderer and the huntsman-detective." 1914: Anarchist Mikhail Bakunin b. near Moscow, to aristocratic parents.

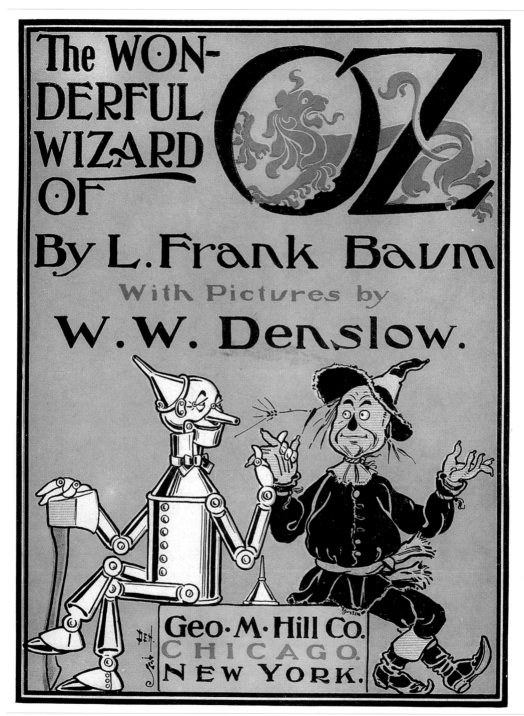

1868: Dostoyevsky's first child is baptized, and she dies eight days later of pneumonia. The heartstricken father had earlier written that the child resembled him "right down to the wrinkles on my forehead—there she lies [in her cradle] as if she were working on a novel!" 1930: Lorraine Hansberry b. Chicago. 1952: Lillian Hellman refuses to testify against her associates before the House Committee on Un-American Activities: "I cannot and will not cut my conscience to fit this year's fashions," she says. 1986: "It's like walking into a cathedral . . . it reminds me that what I do in the world is a valuable and important thing."—Mary Gordon on walking into the New York Public Library, in *The New York Times*. 1991: Critically acclaimed novelist Don DeLillo (*White Noise* and *Libra*) explains his low-profile stature in the world of commercial fiction: "Silence, exile, cunning and so on. It's my nature to keep quiet about most things. Even the ideas in my work. . . . When you try to unravel something you've written, you belittle it in a way."

1799: Honoré de Balzac b. Tours, France. A typical meal for the author consisted of a hundred oysters, twelve lamb cutlets, a duckling with turnips, two roast partridges, sole à la Normande, various fruits and wines, coffee, and liqueurs.

1688: Alexander Pope b. London. His translations of Homer were such a success that he became the first English poet to become wealthy by writing. 1919: "You can always get a little more literature if you are willing to go a little closer into what has been left unsaid as unspeakable, just as you can always get a little more melon by going a little closer to the rind . . . ."—Robert Frost, in his journal. 1990: "I have found it is very difficult for people to lie to me now because I am always dealing with the problem of deception," remarks William Trevor.

Lillian Hellman

22 1859: Arthur Conan Doyle b. Edinburgh. 1927: Peter Mathiessen b. New York City.

23 1810: Margaret Fuller b. Cambridgeport, Mass. Edgar Allan Poe declared there were three classes to humanity: "Men, women and Margaret Fuller." 1906: Henrik Ibsen, 78, dies in Christiana, Norway. 1907: Rudyard Kipling, 42, becomes the youngest winner of the Nobel Prize for Literature.

24 1861: Ivan Turgenev has Leo Tolstoy to his house to read the proofs of *Fathers and Sons*—and watches while Tolstoy falls asleep after glancing at a few pages. 1940: Joseph Brodsky b. Leningrad. He has said, "Twentieth-century Russian literature has produced nothing special except perhaps one novel and two stories by Andrei Platonov, who ended his days sweeping streets." 1966: C. Day Lewis tells the *Christian Science Monitor,* "No good poem, however confessional it may be, is just a self-expression. Who on earth would claim that the pearl *expresses* the oyster?" 1990: On the publication of *The Buddha of Suburbia,* a roman à clef about coming of age in 1970s London, Hanif Kureishi (*My Beautiful Launderette*) reflects on earlier years as a hot young playwright: "They liked me because I was Indian, and lower-middle class. *That* was chic. And I was pretty—then."

25 1803: Ralph Waldo Emerson b. Boston. 1911: Thomas Mann visits the Lido and gets the inspiration for *Death in Venice.* 1927: Robert Ludlum b. New York City.

1991: A. S. Byatt, author of *Possession,* comments on the contemporary British literary landscape: "There is a generation of Martin Amis admirers who feel it's their duty to report on the terrible seamy side of Thatcher's Britain. . . . Then, you see, you get A. N. Wilson reviving Barbara Pym as if she was a figure of any importance. She *isn't.* Then there are people like Julian Barnes, who don't fit into either category . . . although I'm not really sure what he's saying."

1867: Arnold Bennett b. Staffordshire, England. In reference to Bennett's fascination with money, Ezra Pound later calls him "Nickel cash-register Bennett" and Wyndham Lewis calls him "the Hitler of the book racket." 1894: Dashiell Hammett b. St. Mary's County, Md. 1907: Rachel Carson b. Springdale, Pa. She would say, "The discipline of the writer is to learn to be still and listen to what his subject has to tell him." 1912: John Cheever b. Quincy, Mass. His definition of a good editor was "a man I think charming, who sends me large checks, praises my work, my physical beauty, and my sexual prowess, and who has a stranglehold on the publisher and the bank." 1915: Herman Wouk b. New York City. "I regard the writing of humor as a supreme artistic challenge," he once remarked. 1930: John Barth b. Cambridge, Md. "Reading is as private as thinking or dreaming, exactly," he observed. "One imagines that it will be valued (and permitted) as long as private thinking and dreaming are valued and permitted."

Left: Dashiell Hammett *Right:* John Cheever

1908: Ian Fleming b. London. In a letter to Raymond Chandler, he once wrote: "You, after all, write 'novels of suspense' . . . if not sociological studies—whereas my books are straight pillow fantasies of the bang-bang, kiss-kiss variety." 1916: Walker Percy b. Birmingham, Ala.

1874: G. K. Chesterton b. London. 1906: T. H. White b. Bombay. His writing was called "a shake-up of Evelyn Waugh, Laurel and Hardy, John Erskine, and the Marquis de Sade." 1986: "It takes a lot of energy and a lot of neurosis to write a novel . . . if you were really sensible, you'd do something else."—Lawrence Durrell, in *The Washington Post*.

1903: Countee Cullen b. New York City. 1960: "When I stop [working] the rest of the day is posthumous," Tennessee Williams tells the *Pittsburgh Press*. "I'm only really alive when I'm writing."

1669: Beset by failing eyesight, Samuel Pepys concludes his famous *Diary* at 36 years old. 1819: Walt Whitman b. West Hills, N.Y. He later self-published the first editions of *Leaves of Grass*, writing his own reviews and describing himself as "of pure American breed, large and lusty, a naive, masculine, affectionate, contemplative, sensual, imperious person." 1858: "A thing that has been written all at once cannot be ripe. They say there was not a blot on Shakespeare's manuscripts. That is why there are so many enormities and so much bad taste in him; he would have done much better if he had worked harder."—Fyodor Dostoyevsky to his brother.

JUNE

1825: Emily Brontë leaves Cowan Bridge School, which marks in its record book: "Subsequent career—governess." 1958: On his eightieth birthday, John Masefield tells *The New York Times*, "In the power and splendor of the universe, inspiration waits for the millions to come. Man has only to strive for it. Poems greater than the *Illiad*, plays greater than *Macbeth*, stories more engaging than *Don Quixote* await their seeker and finder."

1840: Thomas Hardy b. Dorchester, England. His *Jude the Obscure* (1895) was greeted with a torrent of bile. Critics called it "dirt, drivel and damnation," Irish novelist George Moore called Hardy "an abortion of George Eliot," and a bishop actually burned his copy of the book and sent Hardy the ashes. 1913: Barbara Pym b. Shropshire, England.

1926: Allen Ginsberg b. Newark, N.J. 1936: Larry McMurtry b. Wichita Falls, Tex. 1964: T. S. Eliot writes to Groucho Marx: "The picture of you in the newspaper saying that, amongst other reasons, you have come to London to see me has greatly enhanced my credit line in the neighborhood, and particularly with the greengrocer across the street."

Opposite: Allen Ginsberg *Right:* T. S. Eliot

1940: *The Heart Is a Lonely Hunter* by 23-year-old Carson McCullers is published.

1884: Ivy Compton-Burnett b. London. When *The Times* (London) asked her in 1969 about her life, she responded, "There isn't much to say. I haven't been at all deedy." **1898:** Federico Garcia Lorca b. Fuentrevaquero, Spain. **1988:** On the thirtieth anniversary of the publication of Nabokov's *Lolita*, Erica Jong compares its reception to that given her own controversial debut, *Fear of Flying:* "Much as one wants the acceptance conferred by bestsellerdom, it is bittersweet to win this by being thought a pervert . . . "

1606: Pierre Corneille b. Rouen, France. **1799:** Aleksandr Pushkin b. Moscow. The poet was so popular among the Russian people that when he was killed in 1837 in a duel over his wife, his body had to be smuggled out of Moscow to prevent rioting at his funeral. **1875:** Thomas Mann b. Lübeck, Germany. He once said, "A writer is somebody for whom writing is more difficult than it is for other people." **1925:** Maxine Kumin b. Philadelphia. In *Living Alone with Jesus* (1972), the poet wrote: "Can it be/I am the only Jew residing in Danville, Kentucky/looking for matzoh in the Safeway and the A&P?" **1939:** "On the hottest day of the year I saw two nuns buying a typewriter in Selfridges. Oh, what were they going to do with it?"—Barbara Pym, in her journal.

1899: Elizabeth Bowen b. Dublin. **1930:** Dashiell Hammett, distraught by the inaccuracies he encountered in mystery fiction, published twenty-four "suggestions that might be of value to somebody" in the *New York Evening Post*. His tips included: "It is impossible to see anything by the flash of an ordinary gun, though it is easy to imagine you have seen things" and "'Youse' is the plural of 'you.'" **1943:** Nikki Giovanni b. Knoxville, Tenn. In *Spin a Soft Black Song*, she wrote: "You could say we've lost our innocence. That's a little worse than losing the nickel to put in Sunday school, though not quite as bad as losing the dime for ice cream afterward." **1987:** Scott Turow receives $200,000 and sells the film rights for his first novel, *Presumed Innocent*, for $1 million before the book is even written.

8 1374: Geoffrey Chaucer is named Comptroller of the Customs and Subsidy of Wools at a salary of £10 a year.

9 1922: Dramatist George Axelrod (*The Seven Year Itch* and *Breakfast at Tiffany's*) b. New York City.

10 1919: "I have discovered that I cannot burn the candle at one end and write a book with the other."—Katherine Mansfield, in her journal. 1928: Maurice Sendak b. Brooklyn. "You cannot write for children. . . . They're much too complicated. You can only write books that are of interest to them," he told *The Boston Globe*.

11 1575: Ben Jonson b. London. 1899: Yasunari Kawabata b. Osaka, Japan. In 1968, he will become the first Japanese to win the Nobel Prize for Literature. 1925: William Styron b. Newport News, Va. As an editorial assistant for McGraw-Hill in 1947, he rejected Thor Heyerdahl's *Kon-Tiki*, which became a best-seller for Rand McNally three years later. "If McGraw-Hill had paid me more than 90 cents an hour," Styron later said, "I might have been more sensitive to the nexus between good books and filthy lucre." 1959: The United States bans D. H. Lawrence's *Lady Chatterley's Lover*. Nine months later the ban is lifted.

1892: Djuna Barnes b. Cornwall-on-Hudson, N.Y. 1929: Anne Frank b. Frankfurt-am-Main, Germany. 1985: "A good heavy book holds you down. It's an anchor that keeps you from getting up and having another gin and tonic."—Roy Blount, Jr., in *The New York Times.*

1752: Fanny Burney b. King's Lynn, England. 1865: W. B. Yeats b. Dublin. His son Michael would later recall his father's "state" when working on a poem: "He'd make a low, tuneless hum and his hand would start beating time. . . . He was oblivious to everything else. Once he was on the bus from Dublin and my sister, Anne, got on. . . . When they got out at our gate, he looked at her vaguely and said, 'Oh, who is it you wish to see?'" 1893: Dorothy Sayers b. Oxford, England. In 1956's *Clouds of Witness*, she wrote, "Well-bred English people never have imagination." 1960: Boris Pasternak tells *Life* magazine, "Poetry is a rich, full-bodied whistle, cracked ice crunching in pails, the night that numbs the leaf, the duel of two nightingales, the sweet pea that has run wild. Creation's tears in shoulder blades."

1811: Harriet Beecher Stowe b. Litchfield, Conn. Her *Uncle Tom's Cabin* was the first American novel to sell more than a million copies. 1933: Jerzy Kosinski b. Lodz, Poland. 1963: Dorothy Parker wakes up to find husband Alan Campbell dead beside her. When a neighbor asks if she can get her anything, Parker replies, "A new husband." When the neighbor upbraids her for her callousness, Parker sighs, "So sorry. Then run down to the corner and get me a ham and cheese on rye and hold the mayo."

W. B. Yeats

1902: Erik Erikson (born Erik Homburger) b. Frankfurt-am-Main, Germany.

1904: "Bloomsday," the day on which the events of Joyce's *Ulysses* transpire. It is still celebrated annually with marathon readings from the book in Dublin and New York City. 1938: Joyce Carol Oates b. Lockport, N.Y. 1991: "Gay writers have been liberated by the extremity of their situation," writes Edmund White (*A Boy's Own Story* and *The Beautiful Room Is Empty*). "The reticence you find in, say, a Raymond Carver story about a troubled marriage just isn't meaningful to a gay writer, who finds himself faced with a whole constellation of relationships . . . that have almost never been described before." 1991: After the break-up of a seventeen-year relationship, best-selling author Rona Jaffe gives women tips on looking for Mr. Right: "Watch how he treats his mother, his child, his dog, the people in his little satellite who are emotionally dependent on him. Not his friends, because sometimes he's nicer to them than you."

© JILL KREMENTZ

1914: John Hersey b. Tianjin, China. In 1950, he said to *Time* magazine, "Journalism allows its readers to witness history; fiction gives its readers an opportunity to live it." 1917: Gwendolyn Brooks b. Topeka, Kans. Her *Annie Allen* earned her a Pulizer Prize in 1950, making her the first African-American to win the prize.

Joyce Carol Oates

1898: A *New York Times* critic dismisses the burgeoning career of George Bernard Shaw, calling him "This voluble Jack-of-all-Trades. . . . This carnivorous vegetarian." 1937: Gail Godwin b. Birmingham, Ala. "The prospect of people reading my diaries after I am dead does not disturb me in the least," she wrote. "I like to think of pooling myself with other introspective hearts: madmen (and women), prudes, profligates, celebrities, outcasts, heroes, artists, saints, the lovelorn and the lucky, the foolish and the proud."

1623: Blaise Pascal b. Clermont-Ferrand, France. "If the nose of Cleopatra had been shorter, the whole face of the earth would have been changed," he later wrote in his famous *Pensées*. 1947: Salman Rushdie b. Bombay, India. 1965: The story "Hapworth 16, 1924" appears in *The New Yorker*, the last writing that the reclusive J. D. Salinger has published to date.

1865: Walt Whitman takes a post in the Attorney General's Office in Washington, D.C., having been discharged from his position in the Department of the Interior because of the outcry over *Leaves of Grass.* 1905: Lillian Hellman b. New Orleans. In 1980, Mary McCarthy would call her "a dishonest writer . . . every word she writes is a lie, including 'and' and 'the' . . ." Hellman instituted a $2.25 million defamation suit against McCarthy but died before the case came to trial.

1905: Jean-Paul Sartre b. Paris. He declined the Nobel Prize for Literature in 1964, the only author ever to do so, saying: "A writer must refuse to allow himself to be transformed into an institution." 1912: Mary McCarthy b. Seattle, Wash. Of reviewers, she said, "To be disesteemed by people you don't have much respect for is not the worst fate." 1935: Françoise Sagan b. Cajarc, France.

1898: Erich Maria Remarque (*All Quiet on the Western Front*) b. Westphalia, Germany. 1906: Anne Morrow Lindbergh b. Englewood, N.J.

Mary McCarthy

1889: Russian poet Anna Akhmatova b. Bolshoy Fontan, near Odessa. Her creative life begins before the Bolshevik Revolution and continues well into the 1960s.

1842: Ambrose Bierce b. Meigs County, Ohio. 1961: John Ciardi b. Boston. "You don't have to suffer to be a poet," he once said. "Adolescence is enough suffering for anyone."

1903: George Orwell b. Bengal, India. Cyril Connolly later says of him that "he would not blow his nose without moralising on conditions in the handkerchief industry."

1892: Pearl S. Buck b. Hillsboro, W.Va. "In a mood of faith and hope my work goes on," the author of the best-selling *The Good Earth* once wrote. "A ream of fresh paper lies on my desk waiting for the next book. I am a writer and I take up my pen to write."

1872: Paul Laurence Dunbar b. Dayton, Ohio. 1880: Helen Keller b. Tuscumbia, Ala. In *The Story of My Life* (1903), the blind and deaf author wrote, "Everthing has its wonders, even darkness and silence, and I learn, whatever state I may be in, therein to be content." 1926: Frank O'Hara b. Baltimore, Md. 1987: "The pleasure of writing, in practice, is that of eating a nice, juicy steak with loose teeth."—Roy Blount, Jr., in his journal. 1991: "In Provence, the people are more open than in Paris. . . . Even if they are superficial, it's much more pleasant to be greeted by a friendly superficiality than a stern face."— Peter Mayle, author of *A Year in Provence.*

1712: Jean-Jacques Rousseau b. Geneva. His 1761 novel *Julie, ou La Nouvelle Héloïse* was so popular that copies could not be printed fast enough, and readers rented it from owners for twelve sous an hour. 1867: Luigi Pirandello (*Six Characters in Search of an Author*) b. Sicily. The playwright will win the Nobel Prize for Literature in 1934.

1613: The Globe Theatre in London burns to the ground during a performance of Shakespeare's *Henry VIII.* 1900: Antoine de Saint-Exupéry b. Lyons, France.

1911: Czeslaw Milosz b. near Vilna, Lithuania. The poet will win the Nobel Prize for Literature in 1980. 1936: Margaret Mitchell's *Gone With the Wind* is published by Macmillan and becomes the fastest-selling novel in U. S. history. 1955: James Thurber announces, "With 60 staring me in the face, I have developed inflammation of the sentence structure and a definite hardening of the paragraphs."

J U L Y

1796: Madame de Staël writes, "Condemned to be famous without being known, I feel a need to let the world judge me by my writings." 1804: Armandine Aurore Dupin (George Sand) b. Paris. 1915: Jean Stafford b. Covina, Calif. She would marry fellow poet Robert Lowell and, later, A. J. Liebling the journalist. 1992: "I had a good time writing it," declares Terry McMillan of her *Waiting to Exhale*. "Sometimes it got so hot, I had to fan myself while I typed it. Whoo! I write what I like to read."

1877: Herman Hesse b. Calw, in the Black Forest. "Without the word, without the writing of books, there is no history, there is no concept of humanity," he later remarked. He would win the Nobel Prize for Literature in 1946. 1904: Chekov, 44, dies of tuberculosis in Badenweiler, Germany. 1961: Ernest Hemingway, 62, dies of a self-inflicted gunshot wound in Ketchum, Idaho.

1883: Franz Kafka b. Prague. "A book is an axe to the frozen sea around us," he once remarked. 1908: M. F. K. Fisher b. Albion, Mich. She said, "There is a communion of more than our bodies when bread is broken and wine is drunk. And that is my answer when people ask me: why do you write about hunger, and not wars or love?" 1937: Tom Stoppard b. Zin, Czechoslovakia. 1984: "I don't want anything . . . " Gore Vidal tells *The Wall Street Journal*. "I turned down the National Institute of Arts and Letters when I was elected to it in 1976 on the grounds that I already belonged to the Diners Club."

1804: Nathaniel Hawthorne b. Salem, Mass. He once said, "The only sensible ends of literature are, first, the pleasurable toil of writing; second, the gratification of one's family and friends; and, lastly, the solid cash." 1845: Henry David Thoreau commences his twenty-six-month stay at Walden Pond. 1927: Neil Simon b. New York City. 1931: At the Kensington Registry Office in London, James Joyce and Nora Barnacle legalize their twenty-six-year common-law marriage. 1989: Amy Tan explains how she wrote *The Joy Luck Club* for her Chinese-American mother: "I wanted her to know what I thought about China and what I had thought about growing up in this country. And I wanted those words to almost fall off the page so that she could just see the story, so that the language would be simple enough, almost like a little curtain that would fall away."

Independence Day

1868: "One wastes so much time, one is so prodigal of life, at twenty! Our days of winter count for double. That is the compensation of the old."—George Sand, in a letter to Joseph Dessauer. 1889: Jean Cocteau b. Maisons-Lafitte, France. The author and film director once told Ezra Pound, "The tact of audacity [in art] consists in knowing how far to go too far."

6 1886: Beatrix Potter (*The Tale of Peter Rabbit*) b. London. 1954: Louise Erdrich (*The Beet Queen*) b. Little Falls, Minn. 1985: "There is no word in Hebrew for fiction," Israeli author Amos Oz declares. "I boycott that word. It means the opposite of truth. Prose, yes, but not fiction. I write prose, I aim at truth, not facts, and I am old enough to know the difference between facts and truth."

7 1535: Sir Thomas More is beheaded for refusing to recognize Henry VIII as the absolute authority of the Church.

8 1818: John Keats in a love letter to Fanny Brawne: "I love you more in that I believe you have liked me for my own sake and nothing else. I have met with women whom I really think would like to be married to a Poem and be given away by a Novel." 1918: While working as a Red Cross ambulance driver, Hemingway is wounded near Schio, Italy, and spends the rest of the year in the American Red Cross Hospital in Milan. 1918: F. Scott Fitzgerald and Zelda Sayre meet at an Alabama country club dance. Zelda wrote him a year later: "I'd just hate to live a sordid, colorless existence—because you'd soon love me less-and-less and I'd do anything—anything—to keep your heart for my own—I don't want to live—I want to love first, and live incidentally . . . "

Ernest Hemingway

1942: Anne Frank, 13, goes into hiding in the warehouse behind her father's business in Amsterdam with her family and four other Jews.

1666: Fire destroys the Andover, Massachusetts home of Anne Bradstreet, the first American poet to win general recognition. 1871: Marcel Proust b. Auteuil, France. On his deathbed, he instructed a servant to bring him the manuscript page where he had described the dying moment of one of his characters, explaining, "I have several revisions to make here, now that I am in the same predicament." 1915: Saul Bellow b. Lachine, Quebec. "In its complicated, possibly even mysterious way, the novel is an instrument for delving into the human truth," he once remarked. 1931: Alice Munro b. Wingham, Ontario, Canada. She told *The New York Times*: "Anecdotes don't make good stories. Generally I dig down underneath them so far that the story that finally comes out is not what people thought their anecdotes were about."

1754: Dr. Thomas Bowdler b. Ashley (near Bath), England. He became the most renowned of self-appointed literary censors. Of his 1818 expurgated edition of *Family Shakespeare,* Swinburne would say that "no man ever did better service to Shakespeare than the man who made it possible to put him into the hands of intelligent and imaginative children." 1899: E. B. White b. Mount Vernon, N.Y. When *The New York Times* asked him in 1979 about the sources of his short stories, he responded, "Oh, I never look under the hood." 1937: Dylan Thomas marries Caitlin Macnamara, "with no money, no prospect of money, no attendant friends or relatives, and in complete happiness."

1817: Henry David Thoreau b. Concord, Mass. Contrary to his reputed solitude during the Walden years, the "recluse" dined often at the homes of distinguished Concord residents like the Emersons and the Alcotts, and his mother and sister visited the cabin every Saturday to bring him fresh provisions. 1904: Pablo Neruda (born Neftalí Ricardo Reyes Basualto) b. Parral, Chile.

1934: Nigerian playwright and poet Wole Soyinka b. Abeokuta.

1841: The British magazine *Punch* is founded. 1904: Isaac Bashevis Singer b. Poland. He once said, "When I was a little boy, they called me a liar, but now that I am grown up, they call me a writer." 1916: Tristan Tzara delivers the first Manifesto of Dada in Zurich.

© NANCY CRAMPTON

Bastille Day

1796: Thomas Bulfinch, author of *Bulfinch's Mythology* (1855–1863), b. Newton, Mass. 1919: Iris Murdoch b. Dublin. In 1968's *The Nice and the Good*, she wrote: "Love can't always do work. Sometimes it just has to look into the darkness."

16
1928: Anita Brookner b. London. She later said, "It is my contention that Aesop was writing for the tortoise market . . . hares have no time to read." 1951: J. D. Salinger's *Catcher in the Rye* is published.

17
1888: Shmuel Yosef Halevi Agnon, Israeli novelist and short-story writer, b. Buczacz, Galicia, Austria-Hungary (now Poland). 1902: Christina Stead (*The Man Who Loved Children*) b. Sydney, Australia.

18
1811: William Makepeace Thackeray b. Calcutta. He would call Victorian times "if not the most moral, certainly the most squeamish." 1906: Clifford Odets b. Philadelphia. 1933: Poet Yevgeny Yevtushenko b. Zima Station, Irkutsk Oblast, U.S.S.R. In reference to his poetry, he once said: "Everything I do, I do on the principle of Russian borscht. You can throw everything into it: beets, carrots, cabbage, onions, everything you want. What's important is the result, the taste of the borscht."

19
1898: Following the public outcry surrounding his trial for libel, Emile Zola flees France at the suggestion of his lawyers.

1304: Petrarch b. Arezzo, Tuscany. A not immodest man, the author of the celebrated "Laura" poems once wrote in Latin: "It seems apparent that I have lived with princes, but in truth it was the princes who lived with me." 1869: Mark Twain's *Innocents Abroad* is published.

1899: Hart Crane b. Garrettsville, Ohio. 1899: Ernest Hemingway b. Oak Park, Ill. "All good books have one thing in common," he later said. "They are truer than if they had really happened." 1933: John Gardner b. Batavia, N.Y. Both *Newsweek* and *The New York Times Book Review* accused him in 1977 of having plagiarized passages in his *Life and Times of Chaucer.* 1985: "A novel is a balance between a few true impressions and the multitude of false ones that make up most of what we call life."—Saul Bellow, in *The New York Times.*

Saul Bellow

1898: Stephen Vincent Benét b. Bethlehem, Pa.   1971: Aggravating a long-simmering feud between himself and Norman Mailer, Gore Vidal asserts in *The New York Review of Books* that he perceives a link from Henry Miller to Mailer to Charles Manson. Months later, Mailer engages Vidal in a slapping and head-butting fight backstage at "The Dick Cavett Show."

1888: Raymond Chandler b. Chicago. Comparing himself to Hemingway, he said, "I realize that I am much too clean to be a genius, much too sober to be a sham, and far, far too clumsy with a shotgun to live the good life."   1989: Minister, Zen enthusiast, and political activist Robert Fulghum, author of *All I Really Need to Know I Learned in Kindergarten*, reflects: "I don't think there is a hidden purpose to the universe that you have to puzzle out. You are free to give life meaning, whatever meaning you want to give it. . . . I think the operation of the whole universe is a great piece of cosmic entertainment. Not everybody gets it."

1802: Alexandre Dumas, père, b. Villers-Cotterêts, France. He insisted on writing nonfiction on rose-colored paper, novels on blue paper, and poetry on yellow paper. He also had a menagerie of pets that included three monkeys he named after literary critics, and a Tunisian vulture named Jurgatha.   1895: Robert Graves b. London. He said on the BBC in 1962, "There's no money in poetry, but then there's no poetry in money."

1914: Anaïs Nin begins her diary at the age of 11 before leaving Barcelona for America: "I am sad to think we are leaving a country that has been like a mother and a lucky charm to me."

1856: George Bernard Shaw b. Dublin. Of publishers, he would write, "They combine commercial rascality with artistic touchiness and pettishness, without being either good business men or fine judges of literature." 1894: Aldous Huxley, b. Godalming, Surrey, England. In 1956, he remarked, "A bad book is as much of a labor to write as a good one; it comes as sincerely from the author's soul." 1987: Toni Morrison explains that her *Beloved* is not about slavery: "Slavery is very predictable. There it is, and there's some stuff about how it is, and then you can get out of it or you don't. [The story] can't be driven by slavery. It has to be the interior life of some people, a small group of people, and everything that they do is impacted on by the horror of slavery, but they are also people."

1946: In her last words to Alice B. Toklas, Gertrude Stein asked, "What is the answer?" When receiving no reply, she said: "In that case, what is the question?" 1980: "If you are a writer you can locate yourself behind a wall of silence and no matter what you are doing, driving a car or walking or doing housework . . . you can still be writing because you have that space."—Joyce Carol Oates, in *The New York Times*.

1814: Percy Bysshe Shelley and Mary Woolstonecraft Godwin elope to France. 1844: Gerard Manley Hopkins b. Stratford, Essex, England. 1927: John Ashberry b. Rochester, N.Y. In 1984, the poet told *The Times* (London), "I don't look on poetry as closed works. I feel they're going on all the time in my head and I occasionally snip off a length." 1985: "Here I am, where I ought to be. A writer must have a place where he or she feels this, a place to love and be irritated with."— Louise Erdrich, in *The New York Times*.

Illustration of Percy Bysshe Shelley's funeral

1805: Alexis de Tocqueville b. Paris. He wrote in 1835's *Democracy in America*: "If I were asked . . . to what the singular prosperity and growing strength of that people [the Americans] ought mainly to be attributed, I should reply: To the superiority of their women." 1869: Booth Tarkington b. Indianapolis, Ind.

1818: Emily Brontë b. Yorkshire, England. Of *Wuthering Heights*' brooding leading man, she later wrote, "Whether it is right or advisable to create beings like Heathcliff, I do not know; the writer who possesses the creative gift owns something that, at times, strangely wills and works for itself." 1924: William Gass b. Fargo, N. Dak. Contending that "the Pulitzer Prize in fiction takes dead aim at mediocrity and almost never misses," he later said, "If you believed yourself to be a writer of . . . eminence, you are now assured of being over the hill—not a sturdy mountain flower but a little wilted lily of the valley."

1831: Helen Blavatsky b. Ekaterinoslav (Russia). 1919: Primo Levi b. Turin, Italy.

The Brontë Sisters

AUGUST

1815: Richard Henry Dana b. Cambridge, Mass. 1819: Herman Melville b. New York City. His masterpiece, *Moby-Dick*, was a commercial failure when it was published, and in his lifetime Melville was known mostly for his South Seas books *Mardi* and *Oomoo*. "What reputation Herman Melville has is horrible," he wrote to a friend late in his career. "Think of it. To go down to posterity as 'the man who lived among the cannibals.'" 1991: "If we take Government too seriously, we accord it the very importance it shouldn't have," proclaims social satirist P. J. O'Rourke on the publication of *A Parliament of Whores*.

1869: George Eliot begins work on *Middlemarch*. 1924: James Baldwin b. New York City. Fern Marja Eckman calls him "salt rubbed in the wounds of the nation's conscience. He is a scream of pain. He is an accusing finger thrust in the face of white America. He is a fierce, brilliant light illuminating the unspeakable and the shameful."

1887: Rupert Brooke b. Rugby, England. 1920: P. D. James b. Oxford, England. "Detective stories help reassure us in the belief that the universe, underneath it all, is rational," she once remarked. "They're small celebrations of order and reason in an increasingly disordered world."

Opposite: P. D. James *Right:* James Baldwin

Illustration by Rockwell Kent for *Moby-Dick*

1792: Percy Bysshe Shelley b. Horsham, Sussex, England. The result of his tendency to read through the night, wrote his best friend, Thomas Jefferson Hogg, was that "he would often fall asleep in the daytime—dropping off in a moment—like an infant. He often quietly transferred himself from his chair to the floor, and slept soundly on the carpet, and in the winter upon the rug, basking in the warmth like a cat; and like a cat his little round head was roasted before a blazing fire." 1821: First issue of *The Saturday Evening Post* appears. 1859: Knut Hamson b. Lom, Norway. The author based his first novel, *Hunger*, on his own experiences as a semi-starved laborer and streetcar conductor.

1850: Guy de Maupassant b. Château de Miromesnil, France. 1850: Melville and Hawthorne, both summering in the Berkshires, meet and become friends. Melville later dedicates *Moby-Dick* to Hawthorne, "In token of my admiration for his genius." And Hawthorne writes of Melville, "He has a very high and noble nature, and better worth immortality than most of us." 1889: Conrad Aiken b. Savannah, Ga. He refused the honor of being named Harvard's class poet of 1911, and thereafter chose never to appear in public to read his work or accept an award. "He [the poet] had known, instantly," he later explained, "that this kind of public appearance, and for such an occasion, was precisely what the flaw in his inheritance would not, in all likelihood, be strong enough to bear. . . . It was his decision that his life was to be lived *off-stage*, behind the scenes, out of view." 1934: Wendell Berry b. Henry County, Ky.

1809: Alfred, Lord Tennyson b. Somersby, Lincolnshire, England. The Victorian poet once remarked, "I don't think that since Shakespeare there has been such a master of the English language as I . . . [but], to be sure, I have nothing to say."

1971: W. H. Auden tells *The New York Times*, "Art is our chief means of breaking bread with the dead."

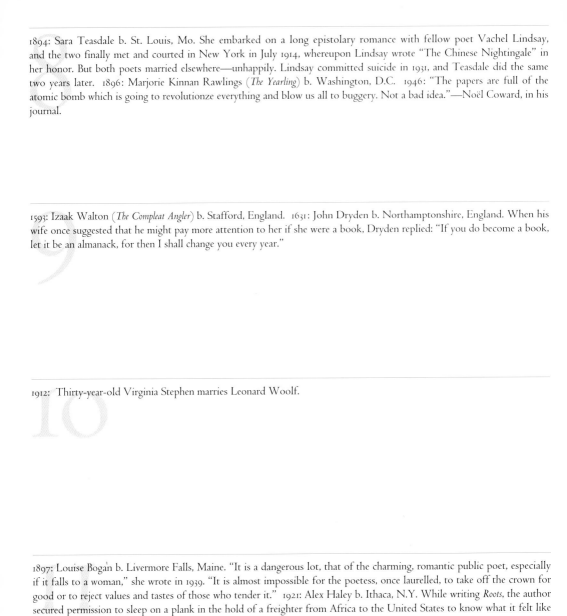

1894: Sara Teasdale b. St. Louis, Mo. She embarked on a long epistolary romance with fellow poet Vachel Lindsay, and the two finally met and courted in New York in July 1914, whereupon Lindsay wrote "The Chinese Nightingale" in her honor. But both poets married elsewhere—unhappily. Lindsay committed suicide in 1931, and Teasdale did the same two years later. **1896:** Marjorie Kinnan Rawlings (*The Yearling*) b. Washington, D.C. **1946:** "The papers are full of the atomic bomb which is going to revolutionze everything and blow us all to buggery. Not a bad idea."—Noël Coward, in his journal.

1593: Izaak Walton (*The Compleat Angler*) b. Stafford, England. **1631:** John Dryden b. Northamptonshire, England. When his wife once suggested that he might pay more attention to her if she were a book, Dryden replied: "If you do become a book, let it be an almanack, for then I shall change you every year."

1912: Thirty-year-old Virginia Stephen marries Leonard Woolf.

1897: Louise Bogan b. Livermore Falls, Maine. "It is a dangerous lot, that of the charming, romantic public poet, especially if it falls to a woman," she wrote in 1939. "It is almost impossible for the poetess, once laurelled, to take off the crown for good or to reject values and tastes of those who tender it." **1921:** Alex Haley b. Ithaca, N.Y. While writing *Roots*, the author secured permission to sleep on a plank in the hold of a freighter from Africa to the United States to know what it felt like to have been shipped to America aboard a slave ship.

1867: Edith Hamilton b. Dresden, Germany. In *The Greek Way*, the American author and classical scholar wrote: "The English method [of poetry] is to fill the mind with beauty; the Greek method was to set the mind to work." 1983: Gloria Steinem announces to *Publishers Weekly*, "Writing is the only thing that, when I do it, I don't feel I should be doing something else."

1422: Printer William Caxton b. Kent, England.

1867: John Galsworthy b. Coombe, England. "The first mate is a Pole called Conrad, and is a capital chap though queer to look at," he wrote upon meeting Joseph Conrad aboard a clipper ship from Australia in 1893. "He is a man of travel and experience in many parts of the world, and has a fund of yarns on which I draw freely." 1925: Russell Baker b. Loudon County, Va. He once wrote, "Anticipating that most poetry will be worse than carrying heavy luggage through O'Hare airport, the public, to its loss, reads very little of it."

1771: Sir Walter Scott b. Edinburgh. When Wordsworth later confessed to the novelist: "I have the greatest contempt for Aristotle," Scott responded: "But not, I take it, that contempt which familiarity breeds." 1887: Edna Ferber b. Kalamazoo, Mich. "Life can't ever really defeat a writer who is in love with writing," she later said, "for life itself is a writer's lover until death—fascinating, cruel, lavish, warm, cold, treacherous, constant." 1904: James Joyce in a love letter to Nora Barnacle: "I hear nothing but your voice. I am like a fool hearing you call me 'Dear.' I offended two men today by leaving them coolly. I wanted to hear your voice, not theirs."

© NANCY CRAMPTON

1948: Anne Sexton and her husband Kayo run into a friend while honeymooning at Virginia Beach and invite him to their hotel room for a drink. "After a short time I was asked to leave temporarily," recalled the friend. "They just couldn't wait, so I went down to the bar and sat until paged and asked to return."

1932: V. S. Naipaul b. Trinidad. **1986:** "I can't understand these chaps who go round American universities explaining how they write poems," Philip Larkin says to *The New York Times.* "It's like going round explaining how you sleep with your wife."

1958: Vladimir Nabokov's *Lolita* is published in the United States. 1986: "I have never believed that the critic is the rival of the poet," Harold Bloom tells *Newsweek*, "but I do believe that criticism is a genre of literature or it does not exist."

1902: Odgen Nash b. Rye, N.Y. He later wrote, "Poets aren't very useful/Because they aren't consumeful or produceful." 1935: "Don't you drink?" Hemingway writes to Ivan Kashkin. "Modern life . . . is often a mechanical oppression and liquor is the only mechanical relief."

1904: The Abbey Theatre is founded in Dublin.

1920: Christopher Robin Milne, the son of A. A. Milne (*Winnie-the-Pooh*), b. London. He later griped: "The fictional Christopher Robin . . . and his real-life namesake were not on the best of terms. . . . It seemed to me, almost, that my father had got to where he was by climbing upon my infant shoulders."

1893: Dorothy Parker b. West End, N.J., two to three months prematurely. "The last time I was early for anything," she later comments. 1920: Ray Bradbury b. Waukegan, Ill.. He wrote in his introduction to *The Stories of Ray Bradbury*, "[My stories] run up and bite me on the leg—I respond by writing down everything that goes on during the bite. When I finish, the idea lets go and runs off." 1979: "For any writer worthy of the name . . . there are moments during the writing process when the rest of the planet might as well have gone to Venus. And those moments are not for sale."—Maria Lenhart, in the *Christian Science Monitor*.

1869: Edgar Lee Masters (*Spoon River Anthology*) b. Garnett, Kans. 1984: "I like poems you can tack all over with a hammer and there are no hollow places," John Ashberry tells *The Times* (London).

1591: Robert Herrick b. London. 1899: Jorge Luis Borges b. Buenos Aires. "Through the years," he once said, "a man peoples a space with images of provinces, kingdoms, mountains, bays, ships, islands, fishes, rooms, tools, stars, horses and people. Shortly before his death, he discovers that the patient labyrinth of lines traces the image of his own face." 1904: Henry James sails from Southampton, England, to visit his native America for the first time in twenty-three years. 1922: "Never have I read such tosh. . . . Of course, genius may blaze out on page 652, but I have my doubts."—Virginia Woolf to Lytton Strachey, after reading the first six chapters of James Joyce's *Ulysses*.

1836: Bret Harte b. Albany, N.Y. When Harte left America to live in London, Mark Twain declared him "an invertebrate without a country."

1880: Guillaume Apollinaire b. Rome to Polish parents. The French avant-garde poet and literary gossip columnist was good friends with Pablo Picasso, who built a sculpture memorial to him after his death on the Paris street now called rue Guillaume Apollinaire. 1904: Christopher Isherwood b. Cheshire, England. The opening lines from his 1939 book *Good-bye to Berlin* read: "I am a camera with its shutter open, quite passive, recording, not thinking."

Dorothy Parker

1871: Theodore Dreiser b. Terre Haute, Ind. Dreiser sparred with Sinclair Lewis's wife, Dorothy Thompson, when the two accused each other of plagiarizing from their respective 1928 chronicles of life in Russia. Dreiser slapped Lewis twice when the author of *Babbit* and *Main Street* publicly denounced him as "the man who plagiarized 3,000 words from my wife's book." **1938:** A jealous Robert Frost throws a poetry reading by Archibald MacLeish into chaos by lighting a stack of papers on fire. **1986:** A small-circulation Soviet chess magazine prints a 2,000-word excerpt from Vladimir Nabokov's memoirs, making it the first Nabokov work ever openly published in the writer's native Russia.

1749: Johann Wolfgang von Goethe b. Frankfurt-am-Main, Germany. **1903:** Bruno Bettelheim b. Vienna. **1988:** "Minimalism disguises a dangerous social agenda," Bharati Mukherjee writes in *The New York Times Book Review.* "Minimalism is nativist, it speaks in whispers to the uninitiated. As a newcomer, I can feel its chill, as though it were designed to keep out anyone with too much story to tell . . . "

1809: Oliver Wendell Holmes b. Cambridge, Mass. He had a peculiarly patrician attitude toward literature: "I like books. I was born and bred among them, and have the easy feeling, when I get into their presence, that a stable-boy has among horses."

1797: Mary Wollstonecraft Shelley (née Godwin) b. London. Her *Frankenstein* was published in 1818, when she was 21. It was her own contribution to a competition between husband Percy Bysshe Shelley and Lord Byron to see who could write the perfect horror story. **1837:** Speaking on "The Commercial Spirit of Modern Times," at his Harvard commencement, Henry David Thoreau denounces society's "blind and unmanly love of wealth" and suggests that "the order of things should be somewhat reversed," in which the Sabbath should be a day of toil and the preceding six days devoted to enjoying "the soft influences and sublime revelations of nature." **1901:** John Gunther (*Death Be Not Proud*) b. Chicago.

1885: DuBose Heyward b. Charleston, S.C.. His 1927 novel *Porgy* was the basis for the opera *Porgy and Bess*, which he adapted with the Gershwins. 1908: William Saroyan b. Fresno, Calif. He declined the Pulitzer Prize, which may have proved to be financially unwise; his gambling habit became so bad in 1947 that he was forced to give up all his property to settle a $30,000 debt. He and his wife were left with one suitcase apiece. 1946: John Hersey's *Hiroshima* appears complete in *The New Yorker*.

Illustration from Mary Shelley's *Frankenstein*

1875: Edgar Rice Burroughs b. Chicago. 1908: "As for kissing—I never kiss but out of devilry—I hate slobber of all sorts." —D. H. Lawrence to Blanche Jennings. 1985: "People have no idea what a hard job it is for two writers to be friends," Anatole Broyard writes in *The New York Times*. "Sooner or later you have to talk about each other's work." 1986: Twenty-five years after his death, Hemingway's family approves Hemingway, Ltd., a company seeking licensing rights to use the late writer's name for jogging suits, sunglasses, fishing rods, and shotguns.

1940: "We [he and wife Vita Sackville-West] are amused to confess that we had never even heard of Bloomsbury in 1916. But we agree that in fact we have had the best of both the plutocratic and bohemian world and that we have had a lovely life."—Sir Harold Nicolson, in his journal. 1957: "I meditate and put on a rubber tire with three bottles of beer. Most of the time I just sit picking my nose and thinking."—James Gould Cozzens, on what he does in his study, in *Time* magazine.

1849: Sarah Orne Jewett b. South Berwick, Maine. "Tact is after all a kind of mind reading," wrote the chronicler of genteel life in old New England. 1926: Alison Lurie (*Imaginary Friends* and *Foreign Affairs*) b. Chicago.

Opposite: Vita Sackville-West *Right:* Sarah Orne Jewett

1908: Richard Wright b. Natchez, Miss. He read extensively from the Mississippi whites-only library by borrowing a white co-worker's library card. On his first visit, he forged a note for the librarian that read "Will you please let this nigger boy have some books by H. L. Mencken?"

1905: Arthur Koestler b. Budapest. "Liking a writer and then meeting the writer is like liking pâté de fois gras and then meeting the goose," he once said to an adoring fan who wanted to meet him. 1968: Archibald MacLeish tells *The New York Times*, "I think you have to deal with the confused situation that we're facing by seizing on the glimpses and particles of life, seizing on them and holding them and trying to make a pattern of them. In other words, trying to put a world back together again out of its fragmentary moments."

1847: Henry David Thoreau moves into the Emerson household in Concord, Mass. after two years of living in a hut on Walden Pond.

1887: Edith Sitwell b. Scarborough, England. Of her, *Time* magazine commented: "In full regalia, she looked like Lyndon B. Johnson dressed up as Elizabeth I." 1909: Elia Kazan b. Istanbul. He once said, "The writer, when he is also an artist, is someone who admits what others don't dare reveal." 1951: William S. Burroughs, later to write *Naked Lunch* and *Junkie,* accidentally kills his wife in Mexico while attempting to shoot a shot glass off her head. 1986: Ellen Kuzwayo wins South Africa's premier literary prize for her *Call Me Woman,* becoming the first African-American woman to win that award.

Edith Sitwell

1886: Siegfried Sassoon b. Brenchley, Kent, England. 1947: Ann Beattie b. Washington, D.C. 1985: "The arrogance of the artist is a very profound thing, and it fortifies you."—James Michener, in *The New York Times*.

1828: Leo Tolstoy b. Yasnaya Polyana, Russia. "I always write in the morning. . . . In a writer there must always be two people—the writer and the critic. And, if one works at night with a cigarette in one's mouth, although the work of creation goes on briskly, the critic is for the most part in abeyance, and this is very dangerous." 1910: Alice B. Toklas and Gertrude Stein take up residence together, "the most complete example of human symbiosis I have ever seen," Edmund Wilson later remarked.

1886: Hilda Doolittle (H. D.) b. Bethlehem, Pa. 1903: Cyril Connolly b. Coventry, Warwickshire, England. "Just as repressed sadists are said to become policemen or butchers," the journalist, critic, and wit once said, "so those with an irrational fear of life become publishers." 1984: Edward Aswell, who edited Thomas Wolfe's *The Web and the Rock* and *You Can't Go Home Again*, tells *The New York Times*, "Studying the mass of his manuscript was something like excavating the site of ancient Troy. One came upon evidences of entire civilizations buried and forgotten at different levels."

11 1862: William Sydney Porter (pen name O. Henry) b. Greensboro, N.C. He started writing short stories while serving time for embezzlement, and later begged his publisher for advances to pay off an acquaintance who threatened to tell the public about his prison past. 1871: "I have the conviction that excessive literary production is a social offense."—George Eliot, in a letter. 1885: D. H. Lawrence b. Nottingham, England. In 1912, Lawrence wrote to a friend: "I always say, my motto is, 'Art for my sake.'" 1989: Oscar Hijuelos muses over *The Mambo Kings Play Songs of Love:* "It's true that immigrant novels have to do with people going from one country to another, but there isn't a single novel that doesn't travel from one place to another, emotionally or locally."

12 1846: Elizabeth Barrett and Robert Browning marry. Wordsworth quips: "Well, I hope they understand one another—nobody else would." 1880: H. L. Mencken b. Baltimore, Md. "In the main there are two sorts of books; those that no one reads and those that no one ought to read," he said once. 1892: Alfred A. Knopf b. New York City.

H. L. Mencken

1876: Sherwood Anderson b. Camden, Ohio. He died of peritonitis and complications in 1941 after swallowing a toothpick with an hors d'oeuvre at a cocktail party. **1916:** Ronald Dahl (*Charlie and the Chocolate Factory*) b. Llandaff, Wales.

1321: Dante Aligheri, 56, dies in Ravenna of malaria, only hours after finishing the *Paradiso*. **1789:** James Fenimore Cooper b. Burlington, N.J. After reviewing "two-thirds of a page" of Cooper once, Mark Twain declared that the author "scored 114 offenses against literary art out of a possible 115."

1889: Robert Benchley b. Worcester, Mass. He failed to graduate with Harvard's Class of 1912 for discussing the Newfoundland fisheries dispute from the perspective of the fish in a final exam. **1890:** Claude McKay b. Jamaica. His poem "If We Must Die," written in reaction to the 1919 Harlem race riots, was appropriated twenty years later as a World War II rallying cry when Prime Minister Winston Churchill read it aloud to the British people. **1891:** Agatha Christie b. Torquay, England.

1926: John Knowles (*A Separate Peace*) b. Fairmont, W. Va. **1985:** "There has to be a woman, but not much of one. A good horse is much more important."—Max Brand, on writing westerns, in *The New York Times*.

1883: William Carlos Williams b. Rutherford, N.J. "I don't play golf, am not a joiner, I vote Democratic, read as much as my eyes will stand, and work at my trade day in and day out," the physician and man of letters once remarked. "When I can find nothing better to do, I write." 1935: Ken Kesey b. LaJunta, Colo. He based *One Flew Over the Cuckoo's Nest* on his experiences as a paid volunteer for government-sponsored drug experiments conducted at a veterans' hospital in Menlo Park, Calif. 1983: "At every street corner, I can think of what the place used to be like. I'm able to see it as it looked before I was alive, to the point where I have a sense of legendary places. It's like an archaeological dig, only it's psychological." — William Kennedy, on why he sets all his fiction in his native Albany.

William Carlos Williams

1709: Samuel Johnson b. Lichfield, England. While working on his great *Dictionary*, Dr. Johnson defined *lexicographer* thus: "Lexicographer: A writer of dictionaries, a harmless drudge." 1980: Katherine Anne Porter, 90, dies in Silver Spring, Md. "I always write my last line, my last paragraphs, my last page first," she wrote.

1911: William Golding (*Lord of the Flies*) b. Cornwall, England.

1878: Upton Sinclair b. Baltimore, Md. 1884: Maxwell Perkins, legendary editor, b. New York City. 1987: "The partition separating life from death is so tenuous. The unbelievable fragility of our organism suggests a vision on a screen: a kind of mist condenses itself into a human shape, lasts a moment and shatters."—Czeslaw Milosz, in his journal.

1866: H. G. Wells b. Bromley, Kent, England. H. L. Mencken said of him, "No other contemporary writer has said so many things worth hearing, though maybe not worth heeding."

1966: "In America only the successful writer is important," Geoffrey Cottrell tells the *New York Journal American*. "In France, all writers are important. In England no writer is important and in Australia you have to explain what a writer is." 1986: Diane Ackerman—variously a teacher, cowhand, pilot, and poet—tells *Newsweek*, "I don't want to get to the end of my life and find that I lived just the length of it. I want to have lived the width of it as well."

1917: E. E. Cummings, serving as a World War I private, is arrested as a suspected spy and confined at La Ferté-Maché, France until December, when he is released and sent back to the United States. The experience becomes the basis for his first book, *The Enormous Room*.

1896: F. Scott Fitzgerald b. St. Paul, Minn. "If the book fails commercially it will be from one of two reasons or both," he wrote Maxwell Perkins of *The Great Gatsby*. "First, the title is only fair, rather than good. Second and most important, the book contains no important woman character, and women control the fiction market at present. I don't think the unhappy end matters particularly."

F. Scott, Zelda, and Scottie Fitzgerald

1897: William Faulkner b. New Albany, Miss. "If a writer has to rob his mother, he will not hesitate," he once stated. "The 'Ode on a Grecian Urn' is worth any number of old ladies." 1905: Sportswriter Red (Walter Wellesley) Smith b. Green Bay, Wis. "There's nothing to writing," he would say. "All you do is sit down at a typewriter and open a vein."

1888: T. S. Eliot b. St. Louis, Mo. He once explained, "Poetry is not a turning loose of emotion, but an escape from emotion; it is not the expression of personality, but an escape from personality." 1992: Eight prominent writers, among them Norman Mailer, Mona Simpson, Barbara Probst Solomon, Norman Rush, and Harold Brodkey, convene at Town Hall in Manhattan to discuss the future of the novel. To an audience member's suggestions of books for a homeless shelter, Brodkey suggests Orwell's *Down and Out in Paris and London* and Rush suggests Kafka and the short stories of Chekhov and Isaac Babel.

1700: "For my part I keep the Commandments, I love my neighbour as my selfe, and to avoid Coveting my neighbour's wife I desire to be coveted by her; which you know is quite another thing."—William Congreve to a married lady friend. 1917: Louis Auchincloss b. Lawrence, N.Y. He once said, "A neurotic can perfectly well be a literary genius, but his greatest danger is always that he will not recognize when he is dull." 1944: "Lunched with Cyril Connolly. E. M. Forster was there. Forster always gives me the impression that, in his extremely diffident way, he is making moral judgments on everyone in any room where he happens to be."—Stephen Spender, in his journal.

William Faulkner

28 1803: Prosper Mérimée b. Paris. 1909: Stephen Spender b. London. Upon turning 70, the harried poet declared: "I'm struggling at the end to get out of the valley of hectoring youth, journalistic middle age, imposture, moneymaking, public relations, bad writing, mental confusion."

29 1547: Miguel de Cervantes b. Alcala de Henares, Spain. He once told the French ambassador to Spain that he would have made *Don Quixote* "much more entertaining, had it not been for the Inquisition." 1810: Elizabeth Gaskell b. London. In *Cranford*, the novelist wrote, "I'll not listen to reason. . . . Reason always means what someone else has got to say."

30 1924: Truman Capote b. New Orleans. Immediately after graduating from high school, Capote moved to New York City, where he got a job sorting cartoons and clipping newspaper items at *The New Yorker*. "I felt that either one was or wasn't a writer, and no combination of professors could influence the outcome," he later wrote. 1928: Elie Wiesel b. Romania. He won the Nobel Prize for Peace in 1986. 1975: In *The New York Times*, Louis Untermeyer advises fellow writers: "Write out of love, write out of reason. But always for money."

Truman Capote

O C T O B E R

1972: "A language . . . is a more ancient and inevitable thing than any state," Joseph Brodsky tells *The New York Times*. 1984: William Kennedy receives the Pulitzer Prize, saying, "Without [a sense of place] the work is often reduced to a cry of voices in empty rooms, a literature of the self, at its best poetic music; at its worst a thin gruel of the ego."

1879: Wallace Stevens b. Reading, Pa. He once wrote, "Most people read [poetry] listening for echoes because the echoes are familiar to them. They wade through it the way a boy wades through water, feeling with his toes for the bottom. The echoes are the bottom." 1904: Graham Greene b. Berkhamstead, England. "The economy of a novelist is a little like that of a careful housewife who is unwilling to throw away anything that might perhaps serve its turn," he later wrote in his journal. "Perhaps the comparison is closer to the Chinese cook who leaves hardly any part of a duck unserved."

1900: Thomas Wolfe b. Asheville, N.C. He later wrote to Maxwell Perkins regarding *Look Homeward, Angel*: "Although I am able to criticize wordiness and overabundance in others, I am not able to practically criticize it in myself. The business of selection and revision is simply hell for me—my efforts to cut out 50,000 words may sometimes result in my adding 75,000." 1925: Gore Vidal b. West Point, N.Y. A *Time* magazine critic said of him, "His reserve of disdain appears endless. He could no sooner shut it off than a vampire could forgo his nightcap."

1804: William Wordsworth marries Mary Hutchinson. 1884: Damon Runyon b. Manhattan, Kans. His name originally was spelled Damon Runyan; by 17 he was a full-time reporter at the *Pueblo Evening Press* in Colorado, where a printer's error misspelled his last name with an o, a change Runyon liked and kept. 1910: Jack London buys from 25-year-old Sinclair Lewis nine plot outlines for $52.50.

Thomas Wolfe

1713: Denis Diderot b. Langres, France. Voltaire, Montesquieu, Rousseau, and others helped him in his twenty-year task of creating an encyclopedia.

1847: Charlotte Brontë's *Jane Eyre* is published in London to instant success. **1914:** Thor Heyerdahl, adventurer and author of *Kon-Tiki*, b. Larvik, Norway. **1963:** Of the Bread Loaf, Vermont Writers Conference, John Ciardi says, "It's not a how-to-do-it school [but] more clearly a confessional in which people who have spent their lives at the writing process itemize their failures while clinging to their hopes." **1986:** Prolific horror writer Stephen King tells *Time* magazine of his nine-to-five workday, "I work until beer o'clock."

1934: Imamu Amiri Baraka (born LeRoi Jones) b. Newark, N. J. **1932:** Zelda Fitzgerald's only novel, *Save Me the Waltz,* is published by Scribner's. In it, she wrote: "We grew up founding our dreams on the infinite promise of American advertising. I *still* believe that one can learn to play the piano by mail and that mud will give you a perfect complexion." **1977:** "My two fingers on a typewriter have never connected to my brain. My hand on a pen does. A fountain pen, of course. Ball-point pens are only good for filling out forms on a plane." Graham Greene, in the *International Herald Tribune.*

1931: Virginia Woolf's *The Waves* is published. **1992:** West Indian poet, playwright, and painter Derek Walcott wins the Nobel Prize for Literature.

9   1818: "I would sooner fail than not be among the greatest," John Keats writes to a friend.

10   1896: *The New York Times Book Review*, eight pages long, is published for the first time. 1925: Janet Flanner's first "Letter from Paris" appears in *The New Yorker*. 1930: Harold Pinter b. London.

11   1885: François Mauriac b. Bordeaux, France. He would win the Nobel Prize for Literature in 1952. 1919: "Success, I believe, produces a kind of modesty. It frees you from bothering about yourself."—Virginia Woolf, in her journal.

12   1990: At age 76 Octavio Paz, poet and essayist, becomes the first Mexican writer to win the Nobel Prize. Paz fiercely confirms that he does not want to retire: "The prize is not a passport to immortality, but it does give a poet the possibility of a wider audience, and every writer needs a wider audience."

1902: Arna Wendell Bontemps b. Alexandria, La. The author of *Black Thunder* would become the leader of the Harlem Renaissance movement in the 1920s. 1984: At a seminar at Manhattan's New School, Stanley Kunitz declares, "Old myths, old gods, old heroes have never died. They are only sleeping at the bottom of our mind, waiting for our call. We have need for them. They represent the wisdom of our race." 1987: On the title of his book *The Bonfire of the Vanities*, Tom Wolfe elaborates: "This bonfire is more the fire created by the vain people themselves, under the pressure of the city of New York. . . . People are always writing about the energy of New York. What they really mean is the . . . ambition of people in New York. That's the motor in this town. That's what makes it exciting—and it's also what makes it awful many times."

Katherine Mansfield

1888: Katherine Mansfield b. Wellington, New Zealand. "Risk! Risk anything! Care no more for the opinion of others, for those voices. Do the hardest thing on earth for you. Act for yourself. Face the truth."—from her journal, on this date in 1922. 1894: E. E. Cummings b. Cambridge, Mass. He dedicated his *No Thanks* (1935) to the fourteen publishing houses that had rejected the book. 1906: Hannah Arendt b. Hanover, Germany. "Our tradition of political thought had its definite beginnings in the teachings of Plato and Aristotle," she wrote in 1961's *Between Past and Future*. "I believe it came to a no less definite end in the theories of Karl Marx." 1988: Naguib Mahfouz wins the Nobel Prize for his *Cairo Trilogy*, his sweeping three volumes of Egyptian historical fiction. When asked how he intends to spend the $390,000 prize, he replies, "That's my wife's job."

1844: Friedrich Nietzsche b. near Lutzen, Germany. He later said, "It is my ambition to say in ten sentences what everyone else says in a whole book—what everyone else does not say in a whole book." 1881: P. G. Wodehouse b. Guildford, England. When asked by *Collier's* about his writing technique, he responded, "I just sit at a typewriter and curse a bit." 1905: C. P. Snow (*Corridors of Power*) b. Leicester, England. 1920: Mario Puzo (*The Godfather*) b. New York City. 1923: Italo Calvino b. Cuba.

1758: Noah Webster b. Hartford, Conn. 1854: Oscar (Fingal O'Flahertie Wills) Wilde b. Dublin. Once, when asked to assemble a list of the world's one hundred best books, Wilde responded: "I fear that would be impossible. I have written only five." 1888: Eugene O'Neill b. New York City. When asked by the New York Drama Critics Circle to provide a welcoming statement on its founding in 1939, he wrote: "It is a terrible, harrowing experience for a playwright to be forced by his conscience to praise critics for anything. . . . There is something morbid and abnormal about it, something destructive to the noble traditions of what is correct conduct for dramatists." 1927: Günther Grass (*The Tin Drum*) b. Danzig, Poland.

1903: Nathanael West (born Nathan Weinstein), author of *Miss Lonelyhearts*, b. New York City. 1915: Arthur Miller b. New York City. 1922: To cure her tuberculosis, Katherine Mansfield enters the Institute for the Harmonious Development of Man at Fontainebleau, France, where she spends several hours a day deep-breathing on a platform over a cow manger. She dies at the Institute three months later.

1899: Fannie Hurst (*Imitation of Life*) b. Hamilton, Ohio. 1992: Best-selling writer (*The Firm, The Pelican Brief,* and *The Client*) and former attorney John Grisham explains in *The New York Times Book Review* why lawyers turn to writing novels: "Lawyers dream of big, quick money. A gruesome car wreck, an oil spill, a fat fee for a leveraged buyout, a large retainer from a white-collar defendant. It just goes with the turf. A nice advance against royalties, some foreign rights, maybe a movie deal, and suddenly there's cash galore."

1931: David Cornwell (pen name John LeCarré) b. Poole, England. "Writing is like walking in a deserted street," he told *Time* magazine in 1984. "Out of the dust in the street you make a mud pie."

1854: Arthur Rimbaud b. Charleville, France. Later in life, the poet spat: "All books are good for is to stand on shelves and conceal the leprous condition of old walls!" 1859: John Dewey b. Burlington, Vt. 1928: Dorothy Parker writes of A. A. Milne's *House at Pooh Corner* in *The New Yorker*: "Tonstant Weader fwowed up." 1985: In response to remarks about the "left-ism" in *Ragtime*, E. L. Doctorow says, "If I'm a leftist, it's because, as I think of them, the Ten Commandments is a very left dogma. What is just? What is unjust? That's where it all begins for me."

1772: Samuel Taylor Coleridge b. Devon, England. In his notebooks, he would write of his opium-induced hallucinations of "moon creatures, exactly like the people of this world in everything except indeed they eat with their Backsides, and stool in their mouths . . . they do not kiss much." 1902: At 28, Amy Lowell writes her first poem: "It has, I think, every cliché and technical error which a poem can have, but it has loosed a bolt in my brain and I found out where my true func-tion lay." 1917: W. B. Yeats marries Miss Georgie Hyde-Lees and settles in a stone tower at Ballylee, bought for £35.

1916: Jack London, 40, commits suicide by morphine overdose in Glen Ellen, Calif. 1919: Doris Lessing b. Persia. She would remark, "The human community is evolving. . . . We can survive anything you care to mention. We are supremely equipped to survive, to adapt and even in the long run to start thinking." 1990: "To write is a relief from life's problems. . . . In art, the writer achieves utopia," notes Peruvian writer Mario Vargas Llosa on the publication of *In Praise of the Stepmother*. "But any attempt to achieve social utopia is bound to catastrophe. If you want a society of saints, the result is hell, oppression, totalitarianism and persecution."

1804: "Dear Sir, excuse my enthusiasm or rather madness, for I am really drunk with intellectual vision whenever I take a pencil or engraver into my hand . . . " writes William Blake.

Doris Lessing

1904: Moss Hart b. New York City. In 1959's *Act One,* he wrote: "Poor people know poor people, and rich people know rich people. It is one of the few things LaRochefoucauld did not say, but then LaRochefoucauld never lived in the Bronx." **1923:** Denise Levertov b. Ilford, England. **1934:** Speaking on "Poetry and Grammar" at the University of Chicago, Gertrude Stein pronounces, "I really do not know that anything has ever been more exciting than diagramming sentences." **1979:** "I can't write without a reader. It's precisely like a kiss—you can't do it alone," John Cheever tells the *Christian Science Monitor.* **1986:** Simon & Schuster celebrates the fiftieth anniversary of Dale Carnegie's perennial best-seller *How to Win Friends and Influence People.*

1914: John Berryman b. McAlester, Okla. **1941:** Anne Tyler (*The Accidental Tourist* and *Breathing Lessons*) b. Minneapolis, Minn.

1963: In his last major address, at the dedication of Amherst College's Robert Frost Library, President John F. Kennedy pronounces, "When power leads a man towards arrogance, poetry reminds him of his limitations. When power narrows the area of a man's concern, poetry reminds him of the richness and diversity of existence. When power corrupts, poetry cleanses."

1914: Dylan Thomas b. Swansea, Wales. "A born writer is born scrofulous," he later wrote. "His career is an accident dictated by physical or circumstantial disabilities." **1932:** Sylvia Plath b. Boston. **1950:** Fran Lebowitz b. Morristown, N.J. She would say, "You can't go around hoping that most people have sterling moral characters. The most you can hope for is that people will pretend that they do."

Dylan and Caitlin Thomas

28 1903: Evelyn Waugh b. London. Malcolm Muggeridge wrote of him, "He was an antique in search of a period, a snob in search of a class."

29 1991: Harold Brodkey reflects on the cult following he sustained during the twenty-seven years it took him to complete *The Runaway Soul:* "It's a way of not talking about the writing. Everybody has stuff they haven't written; everybody has an unfinished novel, or a dream they haven't finished interpreting, and it's something on which they put a profound weight. And somehow that got transferred to me."

30 1871: Paul Valéry b. Sète, France. 1885: Ezra Pound b. Hailey, Idaho. Gertrude Stein later calls him "a village explainer, excellent if you were a village, but if you were not, not." 1958: Boris Pasternak bows to Soviet pressure and refuses the Nobel Prize, only four days after accepting the prize by a telegram that read "Immensely grateful, touched, proud, astonished, abashed." Two years later, he told *Life* magazine of Soviet bureaucrats, "They don't ask much of you . . . only to hate the things you love and to love the things you despise." 1984: "I don't regret the years I put into my work," Bernard Malamud confesses in a speech at Bennington College. "Perhaps I regret the fact that I was not two men, one who could live a full life apart from writing; and one who lived in art, exploring all he had to experience and knowing how to make his work right; yet not regretting that he had put his life into the art of perfecting the work."

31 1795: John Keats b. London. "Poetry should surprise by a fine excess and not by singularity—it should strike the reader as a wording of his own highest thoughts, and appear almost a remembrance," he once remarked. 1977: John Osborne tells *Time* magazine, "Asking a working writer what he thinks about critics is like asking a lamppost what it feels about dogs." 1987: "Twenty or more women and girls, apparently on their way to a wedding, walk along the street pounding on drums. Behind them a dozen boys follow, pitching stones at them. Hostility between the sexes begins early."—Paul Bowles, in Tangiers, in his journal.

Halloween

Evelyn Waugh

N O V E M B E R

1871: Stephen Crane b. Newark, N.J. He paid for the printing of his first book, *Maggie: A Girl of the Streets,* which sold just two copies. Living penniless in a run-down studio, Crane burned the unsold copies to warm a fire in his room.   **1880:** Sholem Asch b. Poland. The widely translated Yiddish novelist (*A Passage in the Night* and *The Nazarene*) and playwright (*The God of Vengeance*) becomes a naturalized American citizen in 1920 and moves to Israel in 1956 where he dies the next year.

1938: "I have become almost piggish . . . not in my manners, for I eat slowly and daintily . . . but I eat too much. Today at noon there was a rich, clear consommé with egg cooked in it, ravioli with tomato sauce and cheese, roast chicken with purée of tomatoes, and brussels sprouts, and a chocolate cream with wafers. So rich! I suppose it is a desire to escape, to forget time and the demands of suffering."—M. F. K. Fisher, in her journal.

1901: André Malraux b. Paris. "The human mind invents its Puss-in-Boots and its coaches that change into pumpkins at midnight," he wrote in 1967's *Anti-Memoirs,* "because neither the believer nor the atheist is completely satisfied with appearances."   **1963:** "A poet's autobiography is his poetry," Yevgeny Yevtushenko tells *The New York Times.* "Anything else can only be a footnote."

1909: Peruvian novelist Ciro Alegría (*Broad and Alien Is the World*) b. Sartimbamba in the Maranon River region.   **1943:** Sam Shepard b. Fort Sheridan, Ill.

1664: In his diary, Samuel Pepys calls *Macbeth* "a pretty good play." **1930:** Sinclair Lewis becomes the first American to win the Nobel Prize for Literature.

1558: Thomas Kyd (*The Spanish Tragedy*) b. London. **1880:** Robert Musil b. Klagenfurt, Austria.

1913: Albert Camus b. Mondoni, Algeria. "A guilty conscience needs to confess. A work of art is a confession."—in his *Notebooks* 1935–42. **1914:** The first issue of *The New Republic* is published. **1921:** "This inescapable duty to observe oneself: if someone else is observing me, naturally I have to observe myself too; if none observes me, I have to observe myself all the closer."—Franz Kafka, about his journal, in his journal. **1989:** "Every day I write more and read less, but I think that happens to all writers," comments 73-year-old Camilo José Cela (*The Family of Pascal Duarte*). "We start by reading a lot and, as time passes, the balance changes. Anyway, I've done all the reading I need to do."

1894: The *Independent* pays 20-year-old Robert Frost $15 for his first adult poem, "My Butterfly: An Elegy," and prints the piece on its first page. **1900:** Margaret Mitchell b. Atlanta, Ga. Macmillan editor H. L. Latham recalls that when he met Mitchell in an Atlanta hotel lobby to take a look at *Gone With the Wind*, he saw "a tiny woman sitting on the divan, and beside her the biggest manuscript I had ever seen, towering two stacks almost up to her shoulders." **1984:** At 23, David Leavitt publishes *Family Dancing*, a collection of nine short stories. "My generation is quite apolitical. We are concerned with politics only when it touches our immediate needs," he tells *The New York Times*.

1818: Ivan Turgenev b. Orel, Russia. The author of *Fathers and Sons* leveled harsh criticism at fellow Russian scribes Dostoyevsky and Tolstoy. He called *Crime and Punishment* "something in the manner of a colic prolonged by an epidemic of cholera," and said of *War and Peace*: "To me this is a truly bad, boring failure of a novel." 1928: Anne Sexton b. Newton, Mass. 1934: Carl Sagan b. New York City.

1759: Friedrich von Schiller b. Marbach, Germany. 1879: Vachel Lindsay b. Springfield, Ill. 1893: J. P. Marquand b. Wilmington, Del.

Albert Camus

1821: Fyodor Dostoyevsky b. Moscow. Near the end of his life, he wrote, "The entire literary world, without exception, is hostile to me—only the readers of Russia love me." When he died, more than 100,000 people lined the streets during his funeral procession, the largest ever held in Russia. 1918: Armistice Day, after which Gertrude Stein and Alice B. Toklas start a civilian relief operation in Alsace, serving there until the following spring and selling their last Matisse, the once-controversial *La Femme au Chapeau,* to buy necessary relief supplies. 1922: Kurt Vonnegut b. Indianapolis. 1928: Carlos Fuentes b. Mexico City. He once said, "In the Soviet Union a writer who is critical, as we know, is taken to a lunatic asylum. In the United States, he's taken to a talk show." 1955: *The New York Journal American* asks Thornton Wilder for his ultimate ambition. His response: "I would like to be the poet laureate of Coney Island."

Armistice Day

1862: "Began writing the fairytale of Alice—I hope to finish it by Christmas."—Lewis Carroll, in his diary. 1890: Two years after her death, the first volume of Emily Dickinson's poems appears in print. Her surviving sister Lavinia had found hundreds of her poems stitched together in satchels and stored in a camphorwood chest.

1850: Robert Louis Stevenson b. Edinburgh. His wife infuriated him when she woke him up from the nightmare that inspired *Dr. Jekyll and Mr. Hyde.* 1912: Eugène Ionesco b. Slatina, Romania. "People who don't read," the author of *Rhinoceros* once pronounced, "are brutes."

1851: *Moby-Dick* by Herman Melville is published by Harper & Brothers in New York City.

1887: Marianne Moore b. St. Louis, Mo. She was furious when a group of friends, including poet Hilda Doolittle, took her writing to England for publication in 1921. Although she later expressed gratitude for the gesture, she still maintained that her writing "could only be called poetry because there is no other category in which to put it." 1986: "The Holocaust is a central event in many people's lives, but it also has become a metaphor for our century. There cannot be an end to speaking and writing about it. Besides, in Israel, everyone carries a biography deep inside him."—Aharon Appelfeld, in *The New York Times*.

Marianne Moore

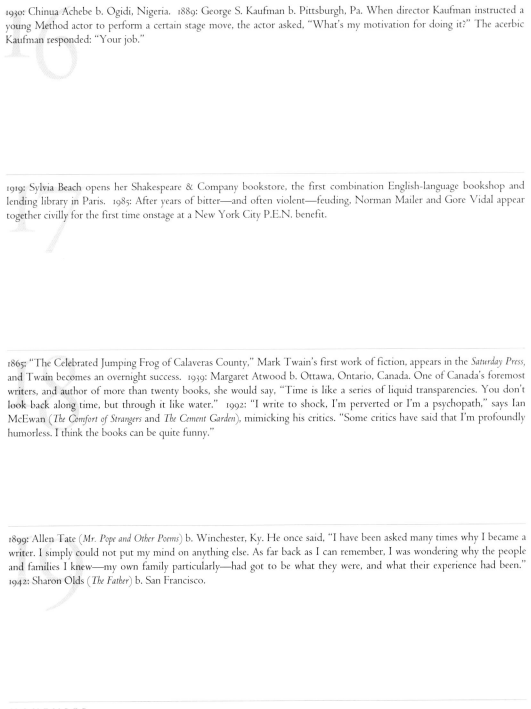

1930: Chinua Achebe b. Ogidi, Nigeria. **1889:** George S. Kaufman b. Pittsburgh, Pa. When director Kaufman instructed a young Method actor to perform a certain stage move, the actor asked, "What's my motivation for doing it?" The acerbic Kaufman responded: "Your job."

1919: Sylvia Beach opens her Shakespeare & Company bookstore, the first combination English-language bookshop and lending library in Paris. **1985:** After years of bitter—and often violent—feuding, Norman Mailer and Gore Vidal appear together civilly for the first time onstage at a New York City P.E.N. benefit.

1865: "The Celebrated Jumping Frog of Calaveras County," Mark Twain's first work of fiction, appears in the *Saturday Press*, and Twain becomes an overnight success. **1939:** Margaret Atwood b. Ottawa, Ontario, Canada. One of Canada's foremost writers, and author of more than twenty books, she would say, "Time is like a series of liquid transparencies. You don't look back along time, but through it like water." **1992:** "I write to shock, I'm perverted or I'm a psychopath," says Ian McEwan (*The Comfort of Strangers* and *The Cement Garden*), mimicking his critics. "Some critics have said that I'm profoundly humorless. I think the books can be quite funny."

1899: Allen Tate (*Mr. Pope and Other Poems*) b. Winchester, Ky. He once said, "I have been asked many times why I became a writer. I simply could not put my mind on anything else. As far back as I can remember, I was wondering why the people and families I knew—my own family particularly—had got to be what they were, and what their experience had been." **1942:** Sharon Olds (*The Father*) b. San Francisco.

Mark Twain

1923: Nadine Gordimer b. Springs, the Transvaal. "The creative act is not pure," the South African writer who won the 1992 Nobel Prize for Literature once observed. "History evidences it. Sociology extracts it. The writer loses Eden, writes to be read and comes to realize that he is answerable." 1984: Lecturing at Brooklyn College, Stephen Spender declares, "There is a certain justice in criticism. The critic is like a midwife—a tyrannical midwife."

Illustration for George Eliot's *Romola and Tito Melma*

21

1694: Voltaire b. Paris. He holds the record for the author with the most books burned in the eighteenth century.

1819: Mary Ann Evans (George Eliot) b. Nuneaton, England. At 38, she wrote to a friend: "Few women, I fear, have had such reason as I have to think the long sad years of youth were worth living for the sake of middle age." 1869: André Gide b. Paris. While an editor at the *Nouvelle Revue Française*, Gide rejected Proust's *Remembrance of Things Past*, saying it was "full of duchesses, not at all our style." He later apologized to Proust, calling the rejection "one of the most painful regrets and remorses in my life." 1992: Julian Barnes comments, "In order to write, you have to convince yourself that it's a new departure, not only for you but for the entire history of the novel."

23

1926: "Fame grows. Chances of meeting this person, doing that thing, accumulate. Life is, as I've said since I was ten, awfully interesting . . ."— Virginia Woolf, in her journal.

24

1849: Frances Hodgson Burnett b. Manchester, England. The singularly upbeat author of *Little Lord Fauntleroy* would write in that novel: "It is astonishing how short a time it takes for very wonderful things to happen." 1859: The whole first edition of Charles Darwin's *Origin of Species*—1,250 copies—sells out on the first day it is published. 1925: William F. Buckley, Jr. b. New York City.

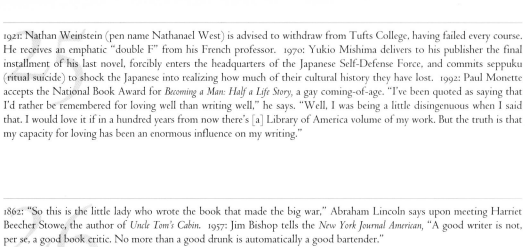

1921: Nathan Weinstein (pen name Nathanael West) is advised to withdraw from Tufts College, having failed every course. He receives an emphatic "double F" from his French professor. 1970: Yukio Mishima delivers to his publisher the final installment of his last novel, forcibly enters the headquarters of the Japanese Self-Defense Force, and commits seppuku (ritual suicide) to shock the Japanese into realizing how much of their cultural history they have lost. 1992: Paul Monette accepts the National Book Award for *Becoming a Man: Half a Life Story*, a gay coming-of-age. "I've been quoted as saying that I'd rather be remembered for loving well than writing well," he says. "Well, I was being a little disingenuous when I said that. I would love it if in a hundred years from now there's [a] Library of America volume of my work. But the truth is that my capacity for loving has been an enormous influence on my writing."

1862: "So this is the little lady who wrote the book that made the big war," Abraham Lincoln says upon meeting Harriet Beecher Stowe, the author of *Uncle Tom's Cabin*. 1957: Jim Bishop tells the *New York Journal American*, "A good writer is not, per se, a good book critic. No more than a good drunk is automatically a good bartender."

1900: James Agee b. Knoxville, Tenn. His biographer later wrote of him, "He was not fit for marriage, only for work. A major writer, he conceded, required major torment."

1694: Zen Buddhist haiku master Basho dies in Osaka, Japan. 1757: William Blake b. London. "I write when commanded by the spirits, and the moment I have written I see the words fly about the room in all directions," the poet later wrote to a friend. "It is then published and the spirits can read. My manuscripts are of no further use. I have been tempted to burn my manuscripts, but my wife won't let me." 1912: Franz Kafka in a love letter to Felice Bauer: "May I kiss you then? On this miserable paper? I might as well open the window and kiss the night air." 1944: Rita Mae Brown b. Hanover, Pa. She would say, "I am a comic writer, which means I get to slay the dragons, and shoot the bull."

"LOUISE ALCOTT" THE CHILDREN'S FRIEND.

Lizbeth B. Comins

1832: Louisa May Alcott b. Philadelphia. Her publisher wisely advised her to take a royalty instead of a flat fee for *Little Women* in 1869. The following year her royalties amounted to more than $12,000—supposedly more than any other American writer had received at that time. 1898: C. S. Lewis b. Belfast. "An unliterary man may be defined as one who reads a book only once," he once remarked. "There is hope for a man who has never read Malory or Boswell or *Tristram Shandy* or Shakespeare's *Sonnets*: but what can you do with a man who says he 'has read' them, meaning he has read them once, and thinks that settles the matter?" 1918: Madeleine L'Engle b. New York City.

1667: Jonathan Swift b. Dublin. When *Gulliver's Travels* was published in 1726, he wrote delightedly to Alexander Pope that an Irish bishop had called his satire "full of improbable lies." 1835: Mark Twain b. Florida, Mo. 1900: At 46, Oscar Wilde dies in a seedy Paris hotel after noting of his room's wallpaper: "One of us had to go." 1947: David Mamet b. Chicago. In 1993, a critic in *The New York Times* wrote, "Mr. Mamet is a man's playwright, at his incisive best when he is chronicling the back-slapping, back-stabbing rituals of males at work and play—not that it is always easy to tell the difference."

1963: "For a dyed-in-the-wool author, nothing is as dead as a book once it is written. . . . She is rather like a cat whose kittens have grown up."—Rumer Godden, to *The New York Times.*

1915: Having suffered a stroke, and awaiting death, Henry James pronounces, "So this is it at last, the distinguished thing."

1857: Joseph Conrad b. Berdichev, Poland. "To make you hear, to make you feel—it is, before all, to make you see. That —and no more, and it is everything," he writes of his role as a writer. **1926:** Agatha Christie disappears from her home in Berkshire, England. After a ten-day investigation involving 15,000 volunteers, she is found registered under another name at a Yorkshire health spa. Christie claims to have amnesia.

1795: Thomas Carlyle b. Ecclefechan, Scotland. He had to rewrite the entire first volume of his *History of the French Revolution* when John Stuart Mill borrowed the manuscript and his maid accidentally burned it. **1875:** Rainer Maria Rilke b. Prague. "There are quite a number of people in the reading-room; but one is not aware of them," the inspirational poet later wrote. "They are inside the books. They move, sometimes, within the pages like sleepers turning over between two dreams. Ah, how good it is to be among people who are reading!"

1830: Christina Rossetti b. London. "Her character was so retiring as to be almost invisible," Edmund Gosse said of her. 1934: Joan Didion b. Sacramento, Calif. In the February 1961 issue of *Mademoiselle* magazine, she wrote: "New York is full of people on this kind of leave of absence, of people with a feeling for the tangential adventure, the risk adventure, the interlude that's not likely to end in any double-ring ceremony."

1883: Khalil Gibran b. Bisharri, Lebanon. In 1926's *Sand and Foam,* he wrote: "I have learned silence from the talkative, toleration from the intolerant, and kindness from the unkind; yet strange, I am ungrateful to those teachers." 1933: U.S. District Judge John M. Woolsey allows James Joyce's *Ulysses* to be admitted to the United States. "The effect on the reader undoubtedly is somewhat emetic, but nowhere does it tend to be an aphrodisiac."

1873: Willa Cather b. Winchester, Va. She subsidized publication of her *April Twilights,* later buying all of the unsold copies and throwing them into a lake. She once said, "Most of the basic material a writer works with is acquired before the age of fifteen." 1971: McGraw-Hill and *Life* magazine shock the publishing world when they announce that they will copublish the authorized biography of Howard Hughes, based on a hundred hours of secret interviews with the reclusive millionaire. The announcement triggers what will evolve over the year into the biggest (aborted) publishing hoax of the twentieth century.

1894: James Thurber b. Columbus, Ohio. He would say: "Some American writers who have known each other for years have never met in the daytime or when both were sober." 1913: Delmore Schwartz b. Brooklyn. 1949: Mary Gordon b. Long Island.

Willa Cather

1608: John Milton b. London. He would sell the copyright to *Paradise Lost* for £10 to his publisher, who made a small fortune publishing the masterpiece by subscription.

1830: Emily Dickinson b. Amherst, Mass. The reclusive poet almost never left her father's Amherst house, and she often refused to see visitors, speaking to them from her upstairs bedroom with the door just slightly ajar. She once remarked: "If I feel physically as if the top of my head were taken off, I know that is poetry." 1991: Art Spiegelman (*Maus I* and *Maus II*) calls comics "far more flexible than theater, deeper than cinema. It's more efficient and intimate. In fact, it has many properties of what has come to be a respectable medium, but wasn't always—the novel—but it has a direct visual impact. Comics can do what drawings do, but there's a narrative."

1810: Alfred de Musset b. Paris. He was so angered when George Sand left him for another man that he wrote the pornographic *Gamiani* about her. 1918: Aleksandr Solzhenitsyn b. Kislovodsk, Russia. "For a country to have a great writer is like having a second government," he once wrote. "That is why no regime has ever loved great writers, only minor ones." 1922: Grace Paley b. New York City. She would later say, "There isn't a story written that isn't about blood and money. People and their relationship to each other is the blood, the family. And how they live, the money of it."

1821: Gustave Flaubert b. Rouen, France. Of criticism, he said, "[It] occupies the lowest place in the literary hierarchy. . . . It comes after rhyming games and acrostics, which at least require a certain inventiveness." 1976: Saul Bellow accepts the Nobel Prize for Literature.

Self-portrait by Art Spiegelman

1797: Heinrich Heine b. Düsseldorf, Germany. Because he was a Jew and a revolutionary in spirit, the Nazis burned all his books in 1933 except for his masterwork, *Die Lorelei*. The poem was so beloved that the people would not give it up and the Nazis had to list it as the work of "Anonymous." 1988: Umberto Eco (*The Name of the Rose* and *Foucault's Pendulum*) comments: "In the United States, there's a Puritan ethic and a mythology of success. He who is successful is good. In Latin countries, in Catholic countries, a successful person is a sinner. In Puritan countries, success shows God's benevolence. In Catholic countries, you're sure God loves you only when you've suffered."

1919: Shirley Jackson b. San Francisco. She stuck a pin in the leg of a wax figure of publisher Alfred A. Knopf when he decided to go skiing rather than meet with her. Knopf then broke his leg on the slopes. 1990: *The New York Times* publishes a defense of superstar Madonna by cultural critic Camille Paglia (*Sexual Personae*): "She shows girls how to be attractive, sensual, energetic, ambitious, aggressive and funny—all at the same time . . . as Baudelaire and Oscar Wilde knew, neither art nor the artist has a moral responsibility to liberal social causes."

1897: Betty Smith b. Brooklyn. 1913: Muriel Rukeyser b. New York City. 1925: "The reason you are so sore you missed the war is because war is the best subject of all. It groups the maximum of material and speeds up the action and brings out all sorts of stuff that normally you have to wait a lifetime to get."—Ernest Hemingway, in a letter to F. Scott Fitzgerald. 1932: Edna O'Brien b. County Clare, Ireland. Of writing, she said, "My hand does the work and I don't have to think; in fact, were I to think, it would stop the flow. It's like a dam in the brain that bursts." 1961: Robert Graves lectures at Oxford: "I believe that every English poet should read the English classics, master the rules of grammar before he attempts to bend or break them, travel abroad, experience the horror of sordid passion and—if he is lucky enough—know the love of an honest woman."

1775: Jane Austen b. Steventon, England. "I think I may boast myself to be with all possible vanity," she later proclaimed, "the most unlearned and uninformed female who ever dared to be an authoress." 1863: George Santayana b. Madrid. 1899: Noël Coward b. Teddington, England. In May 1986, *The Times* (London) calls his memoirs "a triptych in which the presiding deities are Mother, England and Me." 1900: V.S. Pritchett b. Ipswich, England. 1901: Margaret Mead b. Philadelphia. In *Blackberry Winter*, the great anthropologist would write: "I had no reason to doubt that brains were suitable for a woman. And as I had my father's kind of mind—which was also his mother's—I learned that the mind is not sex-typed."

1807: John Greenleaf Whittier b. near Haverhill, Mass. 1913: On his fortieth birthday, Ford Madox Hueffer—later to rename himself Ford Madox Ford—begins to write *The Good Soldier*. "I learned all I know of Literature from [Joseph] Conrad—and England has learned all it knows of Literature from me," he once said. But Van Wyck Brooks said of him, "His mind was like a Roquefort cheese, so ripe that it was palpably falling to pieces." 1954: "What worries me today and other days is that I am playing an enormous deception on myself, and I embark on these thoughts only to make myself more interesting, more complex to other people, more complex to myself. My vanity is so enormous."—Norman Mailer, in his journal.

1870: Hector Hugo Munro (Saki) b. Akyab, Burma. He borrowed his nom de plume from a stanza of the *Rubaiyat of Omar Khayyam.* 1907: Christopher Fry b. Bristol, England. He later said, "[Poetry] has the virtue of being able to say twice as much prose in half the time, and the drawback, if you do not give it your full attention, of seeming to say half as much in twice the time." 1922: Marcel Proust dies in Paris of exhaustion and chronic asthma aggravated by bronchitis.

Noël Coward

1910: Jean Genet b. Paris. In a 1952 interview with Jean-Paul Sartre, he declared: "I call saintliness not a state but the moral procedure leading to it." 1949: Twenty-five-year-old James Baldwin is arrested in Paris as a "receiver of stolen goods"—a bed sheet—and spends eight days in jail.

1968: John Steinbeck, 66, dies in New York City of heart trouble.

1917: Heinrich Böll b. Cologne. The West German novelist and playwright will win the Nobel Prize for Literature in 1972.

1639: Jean Racine b. LaFerté-Milon, France. "The applause I have met with," the tragedian later said to his son, "has often flattered me a great deal; but the smallest critical censure . . . always caused me more vexation than all the pleasure given me by praise." 1869: Edwin Arlington Robinson b. Head Tide, Maine. The poet once wrote to a friend, "You cannot conceive how cutting it is for a man of twenty-four to depend on his mother for every cent he has and every mouthful he swallows. The world frightens me."

1896: Giuseppe di Lampedusa (*The Leopard*) b. Palermo, Italy.

1798: "I do not want people to be very agreeable, as it saves me the trouble of liking them a great deal."—Jane Austen, in a letter to her sister Cassandra. 1822: Matthew Arnold b. Laleham, Middlesex, England. Upon hearing of the death of the endlessly sour Arnold, Robert Louis Stevenson remarked: "Poor Matt. He's gone to heaven, no doubt—but he won't like God." 1962: Accepting the Nobel Prize, John Steinbeck says, "I am impelled not to squeak like a grateful and apologetic mouse, but to roar like a lion out of pride in my profession."

1711: Dorothy Wordsworth b. Cockermouth, Northumberland, England. 1892: Cicily Isabel Fairfield (Rebecca West) b. Kerry Island, Ireland. She took her pen name from an Ibsen heroine she once played on the stage. She later said, "[Writing] has nothing to do with communication between person and person, only with communication between different parts of a person's mind." 1931: Carlos Castaneda b. São Paulo, Brazil. 1946: "A peaceful Christmas day spent in bed talking to people on the telephone. Delicious food, including caviar. Later, a party at Binkie's. Very enjoyable."—Noël Coward, in his journal.

Christmas Day

1891: Henry Miller b. New York City. He once said, "Whatever I do is done out of sheer joy: I drop my fruits like a ripe tree. What the general reader or the critic makes of them is not my concern." 1936: Clare Boothe Luce's play *The Women* opens on Broadway and becomes the hit of the decade, running for 657 performances. 1942: James Agee begins writing weekly film commentary for *The Nation*.

Boxing Day

1906: The Abbey Theatre opens with Lady Gregory's *Spreading the News* and Yeats's *On Baile's Strand*.

27

Henry Miller

1917: H. L. Mencken publishes a mock history of the bathtub called "A Neglected Anniversary" in the *New York Evening Mail*. He plans the article as "a piece of spoofing to relieve the strains of the war years," but almost everyone takes it seriously, and for many years it remains the authoritative piece of scholarship on the bathtub. 1932: Manuel Puig (*The Kiss of the Spider Woman*) b. the Argentine Pampas. 1945: Theodore Dreiser dies, requesting that after his wife's death his remaining estate go to black orphans.

1916: James Joyce's *Portrait of the Artist as a Young Man* is published in New York City. 1988: Canadian author Robertson Davies says Canadian writing more closely resembles Scandinavian than American literature: "I like to think that Canada's greatest writers are Ibsen and Chekhov. When I go to Scandinavia and step off the plane, I ask myself if I've really left home. . . . Even though I've been coming to the States for many years, I don't write about New York. The city alarms me."

1865: Rudyard Kipling b. Bombay. Christopher Morley said of him, "He writes a story ostensibly about big howitzers, and it is really a lover's tribute to Jane Austen." 1910: Paul Bowles b. New York City. 1931: "She lacks confidence, she craves admiration insatiably. She lives on the reflections of herself in the eyes of others. She does not dare to be herself."—Anaïs Nin, on Henry Miller's wife June, in her journal. 1985: "I'm interested in people who ostensibly do have some kind of secure world—my characters are largely employed, largely live together or are married, often have children—on some level they are certainly leading conventional lives. And they're certainly not doing so well at that. Well, that's what I'm interested in writing about—what it's like not to do so well at that."—Ann Beattie, on the "yuppie" characters in *Chilly Scenes of Winter, Falling in Place*, and her other works.

1666: "Thus ends this year of public wonder and mischief to this nation—and therefore generally wished by all people to have an end. One thing I reckon remarkable in my own condition is that I am come to abound in good plate, so as at all entertainments to be served wholly with silver plates, having two dozen and a half."—Samuel Pepys, in his journal. 1857: "The dear old year is gone, with all its *Weben* and *Streben*. Yet not gone either; for what I have suffered and enjoyed in it remains to me an everlasting possession while my soul's life remains."—George Eliot, in her journal.

The sources listed below have been extremely helpful in compiling the information included in this *Literary Book of Days*:

1. *American Literary Almanac: From 1608 to the Present*. Karen L. Rood, ed. Facts On File, 1988.
2. *American Literary Anecdotes*. Robert Hendrickson. Facts On File, 1990.
3. *Anne Sexton*. Diane Wood Middlebrook. Houghton Mifflin Co., 1991.
4. *Beautiful, Lofty People*. Helen Bevington. Harcourt Brace Jovanovich, 1946, 1974.
5. *A Book of Days for the Literary Year*. Neal T. Jones, ed. Thames and Hudson, 1991.
6. *The Book of Literary Lists*. Nicholas Parsons. Facts On File, 1987.
7. *British Literary Anecdotes*. Robert Hendrickson. Facts On File, 1990.
8. *The Cutting Edge*. Louis Kronenberg. Doubleday, 1970.
9. *Faber Book of Diaries*. Simon Brett, ed. Faber & Faber, 1987.
10. *Familiar Quotations*. Fifteenth edition. John Bartlett. Little, Brown, 1980.
11. *A Literary Companion*. Library of Congress, 1993.
12. *The Literary Life* (Almanac 1900–1950). Robert Phelps and Peter Deane. Farrar, Straus & Giroux, 1968.
13. *The Literary Life and Other Curiosities*. Robert Hendrickson. Viking, 1981.
14. *Love Letters*. Antonia Fraser, ed. Contemporary Books, Inc., 1989.
15. *The New Quotable Woman: Completely Revised and Updated*. Elaine Partnow. Facts On File, 1992
16. *New York Times*. The entry date is the NYT date, unless otherwise indicated.
17. *Our Private Lives*. Daniel Halpern, ed. Vintage, 1990.
18. *The Pleasures of Diaries: Four Centuries of Private Writing*. Ronald Blythe, ed. Pantheon, 1989.
19. *The Quotable Woman from Eve to 1799*. Elaine Partnow. Facts On File, 1985
20. *The Reader's Quotation Book: A Literary Companion*. Steven Gilbar, ed. Penguin, 1990.
21. *The Second Book of Insults*. Nancy McPhee, ed. St. Martins, 1981.
22. *Simpson's Contemporary Quotations: The Most Notable Quotes Since 1950*. James B. Simpson. Houghton Mifflin Co., 1988.
23. *The Writer's Home Companion*. James Charlton and Lisbeth Mark. Franklin Watts, 1987.
24. *World Literary Anecdotes*. Robert Hendrickson. Facts On File, 1990.

Picture credits are listed in the order that they appear in each month.

JANUARY
E. M. Forster: The Hulton Deutsch Collection Limited
Lord Byron: New York Public Library Picture Collection
Carl Sandburg: New York Public Library Picture Collection
E. L. Doctorow: Copyright © Jill Krementz
Simone de Beauvoir: © Gisèle Freund/Photo Researchers
Cover of Horatio Alger's *Facing the World*: Culver Pictures
Edgar Allen Poe: Culver Pictures
Illustration from Lewis Carroll's *Alice in Wonderland*: New York Public Library Picture Collection
Edith Wharton: The Bettmann Archive
Colette, Paris, 1951: Photograph by Louise Dahl-Wolfe, © 1989, Center for Creative Photography, Arizona Board of Regents
Anton Chekhov: Culver Pictures

FEBRUARY
Sylvia Beach and James Joyce: UPI/Bettmann
Gertrude Stein and Alice B. Toklas: The Bettmann Archive
Alice Walker: Copyright © Jill Krementz
Boris Pasternak: Cornell Capa/Magnum Photos
Carson McCullers, 1940: Photograph by Louise Dahl-Wolfe, © 1989, Center for Creative Photography,
    Arizona Board of Regents
Anaïs Nin: Copyright © Jill Krementz
Christopher Isherwood and W. H. Auden: UPI/Bettmann
Edna St. Vincent Millay: Arnold Genthe/Prints and Photographs Division, Library of Congress
Title page for *Grimms's Fairy Tales*: New York Public Library Picture Collection
Lithograph by Thomas Hart Benton for John Steinbeck's *Grapes of Wrath*: Limited Editions Club/New York Public
    Library Picture Collection

MARCH
Portrait of Lytton Strachey by Henry Lamb: Tate Gallery, London, Great Britain
Elizabeth Barret Browning: New York Public Library Picture Collection
Mary Shelley: The Bettmann Archive
Robert Frost: The Bettmann Archive
John Updike: Copyright © Jill Krementz
Henrik Ibsen: The Bettmann Archive
Anne Brontë: Prints and Photographs Division, Library of Congress
Illustration by Garth Williams for *Charlotte's Web*: Copyright 1952 by E. B. White. Renewed © 1980 by E. B. White.
    Reprinted by permission of HarperCollins Publishers.

APRIL
Maya Angelou: Copyright © Jill Krementz
Emile Zola: The Bettmann Archive
Samuel Beckett: Bruce Davidson/Magnum Photos
Eudora Welty: Copyright © Jill Krementz
Ezra Pound: UPI/Bettmann
Charlotte Brontë: New York Public Library Picture Collection
Title page for Daniel Defoe's *Robinson Crusoe*: New York Public Library Picture Collection

H. L. Mencken: Courtesy Enoch Pratt Free Library, Baltimore
William Carlos Williams: Eve Arnold/Magnum Photos
F. Scott, Zelda, and Scottie Fitzgerald: The Bettmann Archive
William Faulkner: Henri Cartier-Bresson/Magnum Photos
Truman Capote: © Nancy Crampton

OCTOBER
Portrait of Thomas Wolfe by Soss Melik: National Portrait Gallery, Smithsonian Institution/Art Resource, NY
John Keats: New York Public Library Picture Collection
Katherine Mansfield: Bettmann/Hulton
P. G. Wodehouse: Bettmann/Hulton
Doris Lessing: Copyright © Jill Krementz
Dylan and Caitlin Thomas: Bill Brandt/© J-P Kernot 1994
Evelyn Waugh: The Hulton Deutsch Collection Limited

NOVEMBER
M. F. K. Fisher: Culver Pictures
Albert Camus: Henri Cartier-Bresson/Magnum Photos
Fydor Dostoyevsky: Culver Pictures
Marianne Moore: Esther Bubley/National Portrait Gallery, Smithsonian Institution/Art Resource, NY
Mark Twain: Culver Pictures
Illustration for George Eliot's *Romola and Tito Melma*: New York Public Library Picture Collection
Louisa May Alcott: Culver Pictures

DECEMBER
Joseph Conrad: Culver Pictures
Willa Cather: Nicholas Murray/New York Public Library Picture Collection
Emily Dickinson: Amherst College Library
Self-portrait by Art Spiegelman: © Art Spiegelman
Noël Coward: The Billy Rose Theatre Collection, The New York Public Library for the Performing Arts, Astor,
    Lenox and Tilden Foundations
Henry Miller: Henri Cartier-Bresson/Magnum Photos